THE 24K LIFE CODE

THE ONLY DIFFERENCE BETWEEN MEDIOCRITY AND GREATNESS

DERICK GANT

Dedicated to my loving parents,
James L. Gant and Johnetta Gant

THE

It is possible to live your best life when
you consistently produce at the top level of your abilities.

In order to produce at this level, self-mastery must be developed
physically, mentally, emotionally, financially, and spiritually.

"Be your best. Bring your best. Leave nothing to chance."

Derick Gant

TABLE OF CONTENTS

INTRODUCTION

Crack your code to success . . .

A code is the sum of all the truths, beliefs, and rules that guide an individual, group, or society through daily life. There are many codes; however, most people are tied to a select few by affiliation or association. Kids in the street live by a code. The street code is tight: don't share any information with anyone outside the streets or you may suffer physical or property damage. Guys have a code, as do girls. The guy/girl code is a compilation of dos and don'ts that pertain to supporting each other in an unwritten, unified understanding. The police even have a fraternal code referred to as the "blue wall." The blue wall is one of the ways anyone wearing the badge can know they are fully understood and supported by fellow officers.

We all have beliefs and truths that we acknowledge in our day-to day-lives, but not many people live by a personal code.

There is a difference between living your beliefs and truths and living life by a code. The main distinction with living by a code is the suit of iron society must penetrate to alter your mindset and the path you have laid out for your life. Your code is a force by which you move, unyielding to outside forces or interferences. While society may deem something politically incorrect or in vogue, that will have no bearing on you or your life's plan.

THE 24K LIFE CODE

*"Consistently delivering excellence in order to live
an extraordinary life by any means necessary."*

The 24K Life Code is meant to show you the necessity of having a personal life code and how to structure yours for extraordinary success.

For centuries, codes have been in place to address morality, ethics, values, and even honor. *The 24K Life Code* addresses the actions essential to develop and implement your code for a life filled with freedom.

"Champions do not become champions when they win the event, but in the hours, weeks, months and years they spend preparing for it. The victorious performance itself is merely the demonstration of their championship character."

T. Alan Armstrong

Developing your code is one of the most important things you can do for yourself. A personal code positions the ideas and philosophies that are the essence of your life and allows you to verbalize what you think, believe, and must do. It takes a focused effort with serious intent to formalize and document your code. This book will help you to answer the question, "How do I formulate my code to move my life to the next level?"

Contrary to what society tells most of us, *The 24K Life Code* teaches you how to selfishly become obsessed with the actions required to move your life to a higher level. Some of these actions are:

- Become Your Own Hero

- Be the Star of the Show

- Focus on Solutions

- Go All In 110 Percent

- MAKE IT ALL ABOUT YOU
- BE MORE AGRESSIVE
- GET BIG-DEAL READY
- PAY YOURSELF FIRST

The sooner you implement these actions, the fewer hours, weeks, months, and years you'll waste and the more time you will have to spend in search of the life you know you deserve.

The 24K Life Code is for folks who feel like they have settled in life and are trapped by their decisions. Even with their outward circumstances and commitments in flux, these people have a burning knowledge that a higher calling for their life remains lit deep within. For years, they have put everything and everyone before themselves, and while they are grateful for what they have, they have the need to accomplish more for themselves and for those in and around their lives.

Seeing people achieve and live the life they choose versus the one they accept is my life's purpose and passion. I am perpetually driven to make my mother proud and to live up to my potential. I may be biased, but I believe *The 24K Life Code* is the essential book someone stuck in mediocrity must read. You can accomplish anything with self-mastery, a plan, and an immense work ethic. Within these pages is the information, motivation, and tools you need to help make that happen. *The 24K Life Code* contains the details to set your life on course to raise your value for yourself and within society.

The beauty of *The 24K Life Code* is that you can make it uniquely yours. *The 24K Life Code* is my philosophy on what it takes to be successful, the principles and natural laws of success, and the actions necessary to implement for your success, but I am going to show you how you can use mine to formulate your own code. I learned many years ago that it is best to absorb information or advice in its totality. Once I have finished consuming new information, it is my right and duty to myself to filter it, carefully sifting the dirt from the gold nuggets. The dirt gets discarded, and I only focus on the remaining things that resonate deeply within my being.

Identify your gold nuggets in this book and begin to focus your attention on how you can apply the ideas, concepts, and actions to become the master of your mind. Curiously, the solution to self-mastery is within your mindset. You have to set your intention, establish a plan, and start going after life with everything you have. Given this reality, it is essential to become a self-master to have success. The problem with self-mastery is that the path to mastery is different for each of us. We must become clear about who we are and, more importantly, who we are not. Most people have failed to learn this about themselves. Unfortunately, this ignorance is not bliss.

> *"Every man is where he is by the law of his being; the thought which*
> *he has built into his character have brought him there,*
> *and in the arrangement of his life there is no element of chance,*
> *but all is the result of a law which cannot err."*
> James Allen

Becoming a self-master is essential to being free. To know you are in control of yourself, your situation, and your destiny is true freedom and success. *The 24K Life Code* gives you the foundation to analyze your life, your thoughts, your habits, your goals, and most importantly your actions. These are the essential tools you need, along with your extraordinary effort and focus pushing you toward your ultimate desire: freedom.

Read this book with intention. Setting your intention will give you what you require to jump off the page and into your soul. If you purposely look for answers, they will come while you are reading and/or in your quiet contemplation.

Blessings in your effort.

PART I
DISCOVERING YOUR GOLD

CHAPTER 1
BE YOUR BEST

We all have a cause, a mission, or a purpose in life more significant than ourselves burning deep inside. It is the journey to discover and live out this life's purpose that keeps a few of us in pursuit of our motivation, passion, and greatness. Many are continually asking, "What is my 'why' in life, and how can I live life to the fullest?"

Unlike millions or billions of others searching for their destiny, I am blessed to know what my gifts are and how to deliver my life's purpose. With everything inside of me, I know that I am here on this planet to help people position themselves to discover their life's purpose through financial freedom.

Imagine your life free from financial constraint or stress. What things would you do with your stressless life? Who would you help? What would you invent? What would you easily give to help someone in need? Imagine that the decisions you make daily are free from price tags. People make decisions based on their personal limitations and how those decisions are going to affect them financially. When deficiencies, stress, and financial fears are eliminated, people are more likely to think more clearly and more often. My years as a financial consultant and my participation in thousands of meetings have led me to this conclusion. The number of clients who spent a working lifetime in an entirely unfulfilling career only to profess that now they can finally do what they always wanted is staggering. Are you going to wait until retirement to start living your dreams?

My ability and desire to teach people how to transform their money and their mindset are how I enact my life's purpose. Learning and applying financial literacy and the process of changing your mindset is frankly just too much of an undertaking for most people. People would rather exist in a bad situation than admit financial failure or own a life of bad choices. One reason for this is the guilt of admitting ignorance. In our society, discussing money is taboo. Proclaiming you don't know how to manage money is seen as a failure in the home, at the water cooler, and even among friends. Employers discourage sharing compensation levels, and employees are afraid to say they can't make ends meet. Can you imagine a friend of yours sharing that they have no will power or are simply unmotivated to do much more than what's necessary?

"The price of greatness is responsibility."
Winston Churchill

My brand is The 24K Life. I selected this name to represent the totality of what most people are seeking, working, and fighting to achieve. A 24K Life is one in which a person's desires, needs, and wants are lived at their highest level. To reach those heights, you have to balance life's five core pillars:

- Mental
- Physical
- Spiritual
- Financial
- Relational

Most people are looking for nothing less than the best in each of these five areas. Like 24K gold, to be elite, to be the best, to get the best, you have to become gold in each area.

Golden Nuggets

Using the 24K analogy is a natural because everyone is familiar with what gold represents. It has been the foundation of the world's monetary system from the beginning of its discovery. Every dominant society was built on gold value and worth. Today, we all need to collect and have gold or money in our lives to eat, trade, survive, and thrive. The value society places on gold will always be considered higher than the paper we print or the coins we mint. The more money or gold one possesses, the more choices and decisions one can make about their family and their life.

Pure gold is processed by fire to eliminate all of the combined minerals and impurities. We rate and then value gold based on its purity and mark it so that there is no question about what value it represents. The more impurities gold has, the less value it holds. Like anything scarce or rare, less supply forces the price to rise because of demand.

GOLDEN LIFE

A 24K Life is one in which you strive to be and deliver the purest version of yourself. Overcoming your impurities, things like your limiting beliefs, procrastination, and bad habits, allows you to shine brighter in all areas of your life. When you are confident of your skills, your results, and deliverables, you will become a much rarer commodity. Just like the economies of supply and demand, your talents will be worth more, and you will earn more. Society will rate you and pay you more the better and better you get.

I define The 24K Life as the journey to live your best life when you consistently produce at the top level of your abilities. Self-development must be mastered physically, mentally, relationally, financially, and spiritually to achieve your best self. Complete self-development in every area is essential as you maneuver life's obstacles. Can you survive and stand if one of the five core pillars are missing? Maybe, but which one of the five are you willing to forgo?

Neglect any of these pillars, and you will be at a severe deficit. Each area serves a different life need to feel or be complete. I say, why debate? Take all five and work consistently to get them. Being your best is hard work. If you leave out one area, your value significantly diminishes.

THE BEGINNING OF A 24K MINDSET

Being your best is not about competing with anyone or anything. At the end of the day, any competition is really only from the guy or gal in the mirror. Mastering yourself, the toughest job on the planet, is the actual goal. Very few people understand the relevance and importance of controlling themselves and working their ass off to consistently improve. But you aren't one of them, or you would have never sought to read this book.

"This above all: to thine own self be true, And it must follow, as the night the day, Thou canst not then be false to any man."
William Shakespeare

The interesting thing is that people believe they fully know themselves and have their lives under control. The truth for most of us is our inner child—the kid we were when we were six or seven years old—is running our show; we just don't know it. The adult you is going along for the ride, not knowing or understanding why you consistently do the things you do, feel, and think.

Most of the essential foundational ideas and beliefs we hold were formed, supported, and cemented in our psyche by the age of seven. The problem, of course, is that most of our parents didn't know how a kid's brain develops. There is no magical handbook on how a new brain is impacted and imprinted for life at an early age. A lot of what we were told, overheard, or showed was often just plain wrong. The reality is that most parents just don't know any better.

As far back as I can remember, my brother, sister, and I were all held to a very high standard. I have always been extremely observant, mostly because as a people pleaser, I wanted everyone to be happy. Being alert and aware of my parents' concerns, I could feel the expectations and unspoken demands my parents had for me. These expectations were different from the ones they had for my elder sister and younger brother.

My understanding as the eldest son was that I was responsible for all of the man things to make Dad's burden a little lighter. All of my chores, while mostly age-appropriate, were tough. When I was twelve years old, I was six feet tall. Back then, when you were as tall as a man, they treated you like a man.

Our house was on a corner lot of a busy intersection. During the winter, any time we heard tires endlessly spinning, I had to grab a shovel and go outside to push cars out of the mile-high pile of snow. It wasn't actually a mile high, but to a twelve-year-old, it might as well have been. The year I turned twelve, thirteen inches of snow dropped all at once, and there were drifts up to sixteen feet high. The blizzard was so bad that President Jimmy Carter declared a state of emergency in Ohio and school was canceled. I swear I would have been better off going to school; it would have been far less work. There was no coming back inside until that driveway was free of snow or that passing car was unstuck and on their way.

My siblings didn't get assigned the same massive, gross, or tiring chores. My sister was a girl, and my brother was too young. Lucky me, taking out the garbage and the other chores were all mine, and I was expected to perform them to perfection every time. I clearly remember the pressure to perform in our house. It may sound like I was in a military camp, but in all honesty, it was a very loving home. However, we were expected to deliver what my parents asked, what you promised, and what you were capable of at all times.

Given that we all grew up in the same household with the same foundation, you would expect us to all have the same disposition and beliefs. We are not even closely similar in these areas. As a youngster, my sister was a very independent thinker and would move in the direction she felt best for herself no matter the consequences.

She was respectful growing up, but she was more than happy to move from Ohio to Los Angeles by age eighteen. She wanted to be free to make her own decisions and carve a path distinct from our parents.

My brother was equally independent and would say or do anything he thought or felt as he had no fear of my parents. No matter what they threatened to do to him or did to him, he never flinched. It was impressive to see such an immovable stance in a seven-year-old. I was different from my brother and sister. I was worried, quiet, and always concerned about everything. I didn't talk back, I did everything asked of me, and I certainly believed every word that came out of my parents' mouths. I wouldn't dare challenge them in any way, shape, or form.

The foundation of my 24K Life began when I tried to deliver the man my parents said I should be, even though I was only a boy. I was told to always represent the family with honor and pride. I was expected to be the best at everything I did. Expectations were high, and there was no reward for successful execution other than the satisfaction of knowing you did what you were supposed to do. We didn't get gold stars for chores in my house. My worth wasn't mine; it was my parents'. My value was in my ability to please my mom and dad, as well as the community we served.

The older I got, the more I wanted to please everyone. Being a people pleaser lasted until I took a deep dive into where I wanted to be in my life. I realized I needed to reconsider my value, talent, and skills for myself. I began to understand that being your best and expecting greatness from yourself for yourself is rewarding. That's where every 24K Life journey should begin. My journey of taking the tools, expectations, and successes and applying what my parents instilled in me for myself became my mission. You can have everything you need to level up, but if you don't put those things into action, it's just lost gold.

The Law of Action

It takes a massively focused effort to transform yourself into a person who has mastered yourself mentally, physically, spiritually, relationally, and financially. To master ourselves, we must be clear on what our internal superpowers are as well as the external forces that rule our universe. As you work to learn and develop your inner power, consider the external forces and laws that are at work in our world that you must contend with daily.

There are twelve immutable laws of the universe that represent the foundation of life's external forces. Immutable is defined as unchanging over time or unable to be changed. The definition of insanity is doing the same thing expecting a different result. If you have been bucking an immutable law and expecting success, stop; you're making yourself nuts. In search of your 24K Life transformation, you should understand the basics of the twelve laws.

THE TWELVE IMMUTABLE LAWS OF THE UNIVERSE

- Law of Divine Oneness
- Law of Cause and Effect
- Law of Vibration
- Law of Compensation
- Law of Correspondence
- Law of Relativity
- Law of Attraction
- Law of Polarity
- Law of Action
- Law of Rhythm
- Law of Perpetual Transmutation of Energy
- Law of Gender

While each of these laws is valuable to a successful life, I am going to focus on one specific law that should be learned and applied right away: the law of action, which states that to manifest or create your life, thoughts, dreams, emotions, and words, you must act.[1]

Ignoring the law of action can stifle people and keep them in a loop of mediocrity, possibly because of their fear, procrastination, or even laziness. The law of action demands that you take the measures necessary to achieve what you are setting out to do. Small action steps give you small results, so if you want tremendous results, you have to take consistent, massive action. The law of action tends to be avoided or given minimum attention because taking action most likely means that something different must be done from your normal activity. Many people hate change, and taking action is defiantly going to be a big change. You can talk or desire to be a better person, but if you don't do the work, you will never be able to step up to that next level.

Up until the age of sixteen, many of us strive to do as little as possible. We do what we are told to do, but not one thing more. At the ages of seventeen to twenty-five, we believe there is an endless amount of time and consider ourselves invincible. Nothing is done in a rush because we think it will all flow our way sooner or later.

The age range of twenty-five to thirty-four represents a time of increasing awareness that life is full of potential and opportunity. We see life as a delicate rose to pluck because it's there and we must take advantage of it now. At the ages thirty-four and beyond, the clock enters hyper-speed, so we rush to accelerate our hustle. Life quickly begins to speed up, and everything comes and goes twice as fast.

The mere fact that you are reading *The 24K Life Code*, a book about how to move your life from mediocrity to greatness, says that you are ready to make a change, to move forward, to take action. Consider yourself rare and on the correct path. Finding your purpose and mapping out a plan to master your five core pillars is only the beginning of the steps required to live your best life. Keep reading and continue to build your code and define your value, remembering that massive results follows massive actions. You are possibly one decision away from living an extraordinary life.

> *"When it is obvious that the goals cannot be reached,*
> *don't adjust the goals, adjust the action steps."*
>
> Confucius

CHAPTER 2
SELF-MASTERY IS EVERYTHING

The foundation of your life, your family, and your future is based on how well you master yourself. Self-mastery is synonymous with mind mastery. When you control your mind, you control your thoughts, your words, your emotions, your actions, your reactions, your beliefs, and most importantly, your energy. The result of self-mastery will be that you can achieve everything you have ever dreamed for yourself!

Everything and anything you need or want you can manifest when you control your mind. Focusing your attention on the things you value most without ceasing will allow you to have them. The quest for self-mastery is a lifelong journey, so the sooner you begin, the better. Think about all that goes into accomplishing any task from as far back as your childhood. The things you were confident about and believed yourself to be in control of seemed to happen with ease. The unfamiliar tasks seemed difficult and at times, even impossible. After witnessing someone else accomplish a similar mission, it was still scary and intimidating to you because you had never done it personally.

Thousands, if not millions, of people, have successfully fire-walked over hot coals, yet the idea scares most people. Fire-walking was a test of faith and a rite of passage for young boys coming of age. Today it's used as a tool in seminars and personal development events to demonstrate that what you believe to be complicated or improbable is possible. People who see these demonstrations leave understanding that whatever is holding them back is as harmless as walking on fire. They come to understand it's all a state of mind.

Your mind is a part of your mighty machine that only works if you know how to use it. If you want a 24k Life, you have to learn to operate and control the machine. You must remember and understand that you are the master, you wield the controls.

When you were a child, you couldn't wait to be an adult so that you could be in control or feel like you were the master of your fate. As an adult, you feel like you have no power and everyone else is pulling your strings. Some people never face this conflict head-on and live in fear or hide from feeling out of control. Others take radical ownership of their lack of control and begin to take responsibility and make direct choices.

Once you understand the magnitude of self-mastery, the real key is to identify the tools and strategies to start the process of self-transformation. A great place to start is with the idea or the belief that you must regularly put your mind and your body in a great space to perform at peak levels. Our beliefs are where we tend to operate and they control our lives. Most people want to focus on expanding their potential. You can't start with your potential because it is unlimited and untapped. The measure of the possibility of what we can accomplish is astronomical, but that is not where we operate or run our lives. If you work hard at lifting weights, and one day you lift more than your body weight, you did that because you believed you could. It was the momentum of going into the gym regularly that allowed you to build your belief. You started lifting a quarter of your body weight and then moved up to half your body weight, and rapidly moved to three-quarters. At every level, because you accomplished a new best, your fundamental belief level also rose. Not only did your belief level rise, but your level of fear diminished.

FEAR NOTHING

Belief and fear are both incredible forces undergirding what motivates and drives every one of us. When developing self-mastery, begin to recognize and enhance your own core beliefs. The magnitude of your belief is the key to operating and moving to a higher potential level. The other side of belief is fear, and fear can be so lethal that it kills.

There is no doubt that fear causes people to worry and undue stress. According to WebMD[2], 75 percent to 90 percent of all doctor's office visits are for stress-related ailments and complaints. Stress plays a part in problems such as headaches, high blood pressure, diabetes, skin conditions, asthma, arthritis, depression, and anxiety. Fear can also leave people immobilized and stuck in a pattern of an average existence. Being afraid to fail leaves some people never even trying anything new or life-altering. It is a well-known statistic that 85 percent of the things we fear never come to fruition.[3] The key to overcoming fear is to face it and charge forward. Moving forward in an offensive position adds the momentum of belief even if they are small action steps.

"One of the greatest discoveries a man makes, one of his great surprises,
is to find he can do what he was afraid he couldn't do."
Henry Ford

Small wins or victories are an amazingly powerful tool toward building belief. As discussed, success builds on success and deepens your view and belief that you are a successful person. One issue with fear is the feeling of discomfort. Pain comes with stretching past your current position, during both mental and physical growth. Our mind likes to keep us in our comfort zone, and when we stay in that space, we experience very little angst or discomfort. We also experience no growth. It helps to accept that when you push through your boundaries to reach for the next level, there will be some discomfort. Use small wins to keep you moving forward, but understand this is what you need to be great and to become a better version of yourself.

FEAR OF FAILURE

When we were kids, one of the reasons we wanted to grow up

so fast was to escape the rules and discipline of our parents. Every kid's theme was "Parents just don't understand," a famous song by Will Smith. When I was a kid, I thought my parents fully understood but didn't give a crap what I thought or wanted. Life was structured for their comfort, and my siblings and I were mere pawns on their chessboard.

As a young man, I was surrounded by rules and discipline. I went to a Catholic grade school and college prep high school, so I experienced nothing but rules in my narrow view. We wore suit jackets and ties, and there was hell to pay if you didn't have yours. At home, my parents raised us just as they had been raised, with strict discipline. We had plenty of chores, went to multiple weekly church services, and helped outside the home in my parents' side hustles. I wasn't that kid who played catch with his dad; we were in someone's basement snaking out a drain. Disgusting work, but it made me respect my dad for how far he'd go to provide for his family.

My dad wasn't afraid of anything physical. He'd wrestle a bear if he had to. Even though he was all-out beast mode physically, I believe he was fearful of monetary success. I think he may have been afraid of success because he worked hard but always had little to show for his efforts. My dad had several opportunities throughout his life to take a chance and level up his financial life. I remember real estate properties he owned and pretty much ignored until they were worthless. That might not sound like a big deal, but as a master plumber, he could fix anything. Letting the properties get run down didn't make sense for a man with his skills. In addition, I would listen to dad pass on raising his plumbing prices or not getting paid at all in some cases. This was very telling in retrospect. Why would he let people take advantage of him? What was he afraid of?

As a chip off the old block, I realize he was afraid of not being liked or accepted. My dad was a great guy, but he never had an ah-ha moment with his time, value, or money. Luckily for me, I had an aha moment late, but at least I had one. I have helped families physically move residences and given thousands of hours of free money coaching advice, as well as numerous other things outside my profession. After placing others before myself on the food chain for years, I realized the only way to meaningfully help others is to win personally and win big. Within this ah-ha moment, I had to move my ego aside and accept that there was no way possible for everyone to like or accept me. Part of this revelation comes with age, but the majority of this understanding came from my unceasing desire to make massive change in order to level up my life.

Every day I wake in the morning facing the vision of my greatness. I am not saying this with ego, but with the heart to live the life I envision by helping people who want to be amazing and live the life of their dreams as well.

The 24K Life message that you can live the life you desire if you conquer self and retool your body, mind, and spirit is continually screaming inside my head. It is a voice that is undeniable and persistent. I teach money and financial management daily, but I know without a doubt that accumulating money is the result of self-mastery. Increase your mastery, and you will increase your net worth. Applying *The 24K Life Code* is a way to retool and position yourself to be your personal best. And when it comes to the specific area of self-improvement, you have to face the biggest demon: discipline.

Fall in Love with Discipline

Discipline, although not a direct law, is the foundation of all of the immutable laws or principles. A principle can be defined as a fundamental truth or proposition that serves as the foundation for a system of belief or behavior or for a chain of reasoning. Merriam-Webster[4] also defines discipline as the practice of training peo-ple to obey rules or a code of conduct, using punishment to correct disobedience. This is the critical key. Self-discipline is the ability to control one's feelings and overcome one's weaknesses, the ability to pursue what one thinks is right despite temptations to abandon it. The results of an undisciplined life and lack of follow-through are a mediocre life, poor health, little wealth, and unhappiness.

Every day that goes by that you don't implement your code or adopt a code of discipline is an additional day of mediocrity. Some-thing is going to happen whether you take action or not. Either you are getting more fit or fat; you are expanding your mind or diminishing it; you are leveling up or down. Have you ever seen what a stream of water does to rocks over time? Water erodes large rocks, and eventually they become sand or fill at the bottom of the stream. You are going to pay the price for your life; the question is, do you pay now at a discount or later at a premium? Be warned: the price comes at a premium the older you get. Your minute is not the same as a sixteen-year-olds. "They" say that everyone has the same twenty-four hours in a day. I'm not a scientist, but my twenty-four hours seems more like eighteen. Suffice it to say, there is no time to waste the older you get.

When you look to master yourself, consider that portions of your solution are in your head, heart, and smartphone. What's not normally considered are the habits and accountability you require that keep you disciplined and focused. Once you identify your code or adopt *The 24K Life Code*, you need new habits that are consistently implemented. Creating new habits is easy; it's the implementation part that is difficult.

Did you know that it takes over sixty six days to create a new habit?[5] This means that any and every goal you set should be enacted for at least one hundred and twenty days. We are working on personal transformation. Extra work is definitely in order. If you want a guarantee, do twice as much work. Stop thinking about discipline in negative terms. Look to create a thought process that allows you to understand that self-discipline is just a way of life. Discipline is not harmful in any way; it is the measure by which you get to live the life of your dreams.

CREATE ACCOUNTABILITY

As you transition into this new mindset, you must have an accountability strategy. The fact is you won't be administering any self-punishment for failing to be disciplined so you need to have an accountability system you can trust, and that supports your success. Given your plan and agenda, create personal deal breakers as a first defense against falling into old bad habits. Deal breakers are particular lines that you vow to yourself that you will not cross.

One of my deal breakers involves fitness and travel. Travel at times can interfere with a healthy routine, so when I travel for work or pleasure, I have a rule that I will not miss three days of working out in a row. My routine is to get in a solid thirty-minute workout five out of seven days. I will not go past a second day without hitting the gym or going for a jog. Over the years I have added on to this deal breaker. If I don't work out, I can't eat junk food that day. I call it a double whammy day. If you eat bad and don't work to burn it off, you just had a double whammy. A sure path to the next pants size up.

I also adopted financial deal breakers. The first financial deal breaker was handed down to me many years ago from a business mentor. After graduating from college, I wanted to be the first black Donald Trump. I had just read the books *Nothing Down* by Robert Allen and *The Art of the Deal* by Donald Trump. After finishing these books, I took my newfound knowledge and secured two properties rather quickly. Upon obtaining the properties, I proceeded to drain my savings and even used a few credit cards to replace furnaces and water tanks. The repairs put me in a negative net worth position, and I had used every dime on the vacant properties.

Upon discussing my decision to use all of my resources to fund these properties, my money mentor explained what it meant to have financial barriers and constraints. His main philosophy was never to spend your last dollar. It was a personal deal breaker that he was never to fall below $10,000 in his cash account.

I've adopted this philosophy 100 percent as one of my core deal breakers. As I stretch to move that number higher and higher, I encourage clients, family, and friends to adopt fitness, finance, and moral deal breakers. Self-discipline tools like establishing deal breakers are like a muscle that must be exercised to expand and grow to help us become our best. We can build our power of self-control the more we use our minds.

Never Lie to Yourself

It is impossible to become a self-master if you don't have a clear or realistic view of yourself. As people face the world, they tend to exaggerate their successes or failures just like the size of fish they caught last summer. Every summer the capture gets more dramatic and the fish gets bigger. The continual change in our story could be because we all focus or think about ourselves 95 percent of the time.[6] We are so focused on ourselves and how the world fits into our narrative that we tend to lose a global view of how we come off or are perceived. In society, perception is a reality because it's all the public knows of us. Society's reality doesn't have to be your reality; however, you do need to be aware of how you are perceived.

"When we are not engaged in thinking about some definite problem, we usually spend about 95 percent of our time thinking about ourselves."

Dale Carnegie

I don't think we intentionally set out to deceive ourselves by believing something better or worse of ourselves than the truth. As humans, we have over seventy thousand thoughts a day, and if 95 percent involve how circumstances intertwine into our narratives, we are bound to have an erroneous result.[7] It becomes imperative to manage and handle the thoughts and words that are constantly flowing into our heads. When we lose sight of our truth and adopt society's truth, our whole life can lose focus and direction. The thoughts you feed yourself regularly are what grow in your life, and that is a powerfully important diet. Self-truth is your foundation, and you must have a clear understanding of where you are and what you need to improve to become the best you possible.

Self-mastery is our real superpower. With the right tools, insight, and effort, we can create a life that is free because of the ability to control ourselves deep within our core. Freedom comes in many forms; ultimate freedom is to know, understand, and manage your actions. It is vital to control your reactions as well. This control reduces the impact outside forces have on your mental and physical life. The real beauty of a self-mastered state is that no one can take away your ability to think. Cognitive control will always be with you and in your hands to create or recreate what you will. Self-mastery trumps everything.

CHAPTER 3
BUILDING AN ALPHA MINDSET

The alpha is usually the leader in a group of people or animals. Alpha is also the first letter in the Greek alphabet, and in the Bible, God says, "I am the alpha and the omega, the beginning and the end." I am completely committed and invested in helping you become the alpha of your world. So many people are safely secure in their mediocrity because they are happy followers of average. I say let the people who choose mediocrity revel in it. Someone must lead your cause toward greatness, and I don't know a better leader for that than you. Be the alpha leader, even if it is in your own home.

"You have power over your mind – not outside events.

Realize this, and you will find strength."

Marcus Aurelius

This chapter is specifically focused on delivering the tools necessary to develop the level of alpha mindset you desire. We are looking to implode your limiting beliefs. I expect to expand your understanding of your potential and teach you how to tap into increasing your belief system. We perform at our expectation and belief level, not our potential level, so let's get into the zone.

ZPD

The zone of proximal development, often abbreviated as ZPD, is the difference between what a high achiever can do without help and what he or she can do with help.[8]

In the diagram on the next page, you can see that you are the core and are looking to grow out of your comfort zone into a more significant territory. The next level out of ZPD isn't accessible without help. The beautiful thing is that once you increase your core, there is more help at the next level.

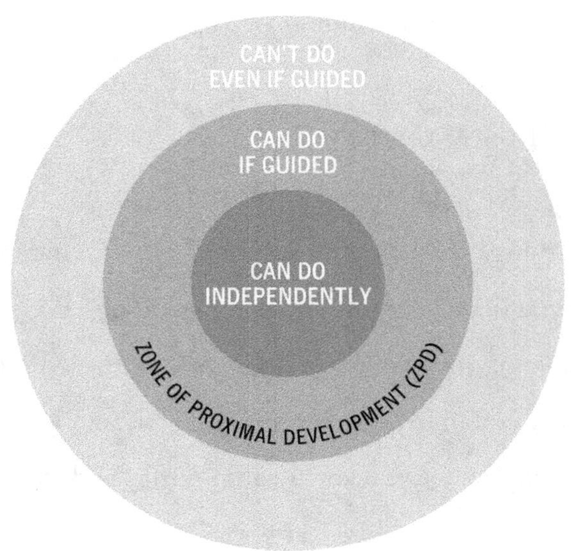

CAN'T DO EVEN IF GUIDED

Inside of you are the things you can do all by your lonesome. You don't need anyone to guide you or tell you what to do. The core area of your life is up to your desire to get things done and to do so at a high level.

CAN DO IF GUIDED

ZPD is the area that calls for outside guidance. You can find a tool, an app, a program, or a coach, but you need some help. You are close to leveling up in this area, but something outside of yourself is required to expand and grow your life.

Can Do Independently

This outer region is out of your field completely. In order to get some things done, you must hire an expert. Understanding this will save you time and most likely money. Being honest with yourself and identifying the things you can't do is definitely a sign of self-mastery and understanding your limitations.

Realizing where you are in your journey and applying the tools you have at your disposal is very important. Growth takes knowledge and consistency. A great tool to add to your disposal is figuring out how to grow daily.

DIAGRO

DIAGRO is a catchphrase that stands for daily growth. I use DIAGRO to remind myself that I must improve on a daily basis to move forward or I will stagnate or move backward. You should expect from yourself positive growth every day. There is so much work we can all do to improve our positions. We need to understand where we are and challenge ourselves to do better. I need a lot of work on improving my inability to multitask and organize.

The concept of making daily improvements is the right way to get better. Consistent growth applies to almost every aspect of life and is actionable in every element in your self-mastery strategy. When looking to make any significant change, it is always easier to do so one step at a time. Getting started can be done by setting a goal and determining what can be done today to keep moving you closer to success. Regardless of whether it's a physical or mental goal, the daily success focus is a great strategy.

Pro Alpha Tools

To build your alpha mindset, you can use several tools. These tools rely on each other and should be implemented simultaneously. These tools are used scientifically and professionally to help millions of people improve their mindset and therefore their lives. Each of the following tools holds significant power in and of themselves and communally:

- Master goals
- Visualization
- Affirmations and Incantations
- Journaling

- Meditation

- Music

YOUR MASTER GOAL

Your master goal is the culmination of your message, purpose, and life's plan. We will fully cover setting goals later. For now, know that a master goal is your most important life goal. Everyone needs a master goal, a plan that sets the meaning and focus on the path of their life. There is no plan more critical past, present, or future.

A master goal is determined in several ways. One way is to define your life's purpose and begin to work backward. A great question to ask yourself is, "What good do I ultimately wish to bring to the world?" You have to muddle through the general goals that, however important, are simply stepping-stones to your master goal.

VISUALIZATION

Visualization is a mental rehearsal of the life you see for yourself or the master plan you are looking to achieve. It involves using all of the senses to create or recreate an event or image in your mind. Finding the perfect picture or detailed vision of what you imagine for yourself is the first step. Once you have created your new story and a complete picture is formulated, your creative subconscious will find a way to solve any problem. The tools and techniques we are discussing will all come together to transform your mind and turn thoughts into words and words into actions.

With the vision in mind, you will know how to get to your desire once you have detailed your process. You will know the how, what, when, why, and where because these are a substantial parts of your vision. Every day you will be walking through the details of your new life. You are striving to think, see, and most importantly feel as many of the details as possible. The more details you create in your visioning process, the more realistic the experience, the more likely it is to come to fruition. As magnificent and encompassing as the brain is, it cannot tell the difference between mental imagery and the real thing. The brain does not care whether it receives images by physical encounters, pictures, or thoughts to produce results.

The most effective way to practice envisioning your future is to find a time and place where you can focus and won't be interrupted. Recline in your favorite chair or lie down, and close your eyes. Relax, concentrate, and focus your mind on your plans. Take deep breaths and exhale on a ten count. As you exhale, imagine that stress is leaving your body. Move throughout your entire body. Continue all the way to the top of your head as you imagine all the tension seeping out of your body.

Open your mind, and work to eliminate distractions and allow your mind to focus on the relaxation process. Once you are relaxed, focus on a specific vision. Mentally tell yourself that you are confident and that you can accomplish this. Tell yourself that you will be successful. Imagine what you will see just before you begin the task. Visualize yourself as an active participant, not as a passive observer.

Professional golfers mentally rehearse putting golf balls. They visualize standing on the green. Once there, they mentally rehearse their measuring routine, their set up and approach, the backswing and follow-through, and finally, they visualize the putt dropping in the cup. When you practice, stay relaxed and focused while mentally rehearsing a successful performance. Imagine going through the process and seeing and feeling the fruitful results. Repeat this step several times with an increased intensity if possible. The more detailed and emotion filled you are the better.

AFFIRMATIONS AND INCANTATIONS

An affirmation is a positive value statement that gets you moving in the right direction when facing obstacles. Let's say you are looking to lose fifty pounds and you have an Oreo cookie fetish. There happens to be Oreos in the house, so you say to yourself, "I always eat healthy because it makes me fit, strong, and sexy as hell." You might do better with an incantation like "I don't eat crap." An incantation is something you repeat to get your beliefs in the forefront of your mind so they can take over the weakness. It's a short, sweet, to the point statement. My incantation is "I handle my shit."

> *"Everything is working together for my benefit."*
> Oprah Winfrey

JOURNALING

Journaling is another significant step in creating an alpha mindset. Just like your goal setting, any time you write something, it becomes real. The fact is, if you tell someone something, often they will hear you and then forget about it. When you write it down and they read and reread it, it becomes the gospel, the truth. Your brain works the same way. When you write things down and review them, they seem to take on a whole new form and life. It's as if your words become stone and solidify in your head and heart. Some people find journaling corny or think it's something a teenage girl should be doing. But writing your thoughts and feelings down is a powerful tool.

When I journal, I am doing it to best understand my mental process and gain control of my mind. Knowing what and why I'm thinking a certain thing, especially things that upset my day, is the path to complete mindset management. Understand your mind and you can better control your emotions. Controlling your emotions allows you to be a better person, parent, spouse, and leader. When you are personally clear, it's like your emotional interactions with others are in slow motion. You see the things that trigger you coming three moves ahead, and this ability allows you to successfully act instead of reacting.

The best way to get started journaling is to set up a dedicated electronic document on your computer or designate a notepad. You will need daily access to write down thoughts and ideas as they come to you wherever you are. I prefer to carry a journal book and pen. It doesn't matter which path you take as long as you choose a way. Just make sure to record your thoughts and ideas as often as possible. Once you have written down your thoughts, ideas, visions, and what you feel, summarize them into one or two paragraphs.

When journaling, I use the Socratic method of getting started. The Socratic method, originally a debate technique, is an advantageous way to journal.[9] The process entails asking questions and taking the time to answer them. Eventually, as you dig deeper by asking probing questions, you get closer and closer to clarity. I will ask myself something like, "How was your day yesterday?" After writing that down, I will ask, "Why it was good or bad?" I will follow it up with, "What could make it better?" or "Why did you give your power to an idea, event, or person?"

If you can answer these sample questions, you will have a solid start to better understanding yourself.

- What am I most anxious/nervous/fearful of?

- When I feel this way, what am I thinking about?

- What about this disturbs me?

- Is this something within my control?

- What is the worst thing that can happen?

- What do I think about myself when I am in this space?

- How long have I felt or reacted like this?

- What felt like this when I was a child?

- What should I be thinking?

- What is the best way for me to move this into a positive direction?

In your journal, you should be developing your mindset in these areas:

- Personal story

- Goals

- Daily goals

- Message to the masses

- Vision

- Mission

- Your why

- Affirmations

- Incantations

MEDITATION

Meditation is the process of calming and clearing your mind. It is very similar to the visualization process with one major exception. During meditation, the purpose is to declutter your mind or unfocus your thoughts on any specific thing. With visualization, your primary purpose is to focus on the exact future you desire and hone in on the details and feelings. You are working to create the emotions attached with that vision while in meditation it is the opposite.

Having a clear and sharp mind is essential to understanding and making day-to-day decisions. At times you have to quiet yourself to clarify what it is you are to do. Sometimes it is easier to understand through meditation. Most people are afraid of what their mind says to them in the quiet. Alphas are not scared. They welcome the new information so it can be sifted and sown into good crops or eliminated. As soon as you begin this process, your mind will be flooded with so many thoughts it will seem impossible to achieve a sense of nothingness. Like anything you do, practice makes perfect.

I was very lucky in my meditative beginnings. In college, I undertook the practice of martial arts. During every training session, we had to sit with our legs folded, body relaxed, and focus on not focusing. The meditation was partially guided, and that made it easier to simply focus on the instructors voice. A few years of forced meditation turned into a life's practice. The best way to start is in small doses, maybe five minutes at a day during your morning and evening routines. You can easily add minutes as your tolerance for sitting still increases. I use a timer to let me know when my twenty minutes are complete.

Understanding how to meditate is fundamental to your success. Choose a spot in your home free of noise and clutter. It is helpful to meditate in the same spot every time. Your body and mind will eventually automatically go into a meditative state because you are in your meditation space. Your selection should be a quiet place where you won't be disturbed for fifteen minutes or longer. Sit down, relax, and rest your hands on your lap. Begin with sitting cross-legged, using support if necessary. You can use any position that makes you comfortable. Regardless of how you sit, make sure your back is relaxed. Then do the following:

1. Breathe slowly
2. Close your eyes
3. Unfocus your thoughts
4. Inhale through your nose
5. Exhale through your mouth

Set your attention to where it should be. As you develop higher focus, you will find it easier to concentrate. When you are ready to end the session, open your eyes and stand up slowly.

Several free apps can guide you to getting started. There are also hundreds of books on meditation for beginners.

MUSIC

Music is a pathway to the soul or your emotions. The soul contains your deepest desires and purpose, and being able to influence it quickly is a vital step to being able to immediately change your disposition. You have to be able to tap into your soul or emotions to be the best you can be: alpha. Leaving yourself exposed and raw, unable to direct your feelings, can hurt if you are either too high or too low. Music can lift you or depress you. There are songs I won't listen to because they are connected to painful memories of past family members. Some songs get you excited and ready to roll. I use music in two powerful ways.

The first way is by having a theme song that gets me amped up. I learned the power of a theme song from my two sons when they were very young. My sons and my brother were avid WWF fans. While they were watching a WWF show one day, I happened by, and they were yelling. They said some guy was about to come out, and they were 110 percent excited. I asked, "How do you know this guy is coming?" All three glared at me and said it was because his theme music was playing. Boom, I decided right then I was going to have my own theme song. Having a theme song gets you ready and alerts everyone that you are coming. I have a theme song that I can easily access on my mobile phone. I will listen to my theme song as often as I feel the need. If I need a big quick fix, I will watch the music video too.

The second way I use music is to reset or change a current poor disposition. Sometimes I am humming along and start to fade energy-wise. The right music will alter that state quickly. I keep an updated one-hour playlist of songs that get my juices flowing and take my productivity to an instant high rate. Building your playlist isn't difficult at all. You can feel the songs that get you going, so just add them to your new playlist. Many mobile apps will identify the details of any song that is playing wherever you happen to be. Click it and add it to your list.

Building an alpha mindset is not about dominating others. It's about dominating yourself! Place yourself in a mental position that allows no one or no thing to dissuade or move you from your mission or position. Every tool in this chapter is necessary for you to dominate yourself and your mind. It would be wonderful if we innately lived by the tools necessary to succeed. The truth is that they are learned and must be consistently applied. It takes extraordinary effort to become great. I'm not talking about what other people consider great, only what it takes for you to be 100 percent in control of you. *The 24K Life Code* gives you the permission you need to be amazing and to live your best life.

CHAPTER 4
WHAT YOU BELIEVE IS WHAT YOU GET

Luckily for you, your unique universe is the only one that you must understand, believe in, and master. I believe in myself and *The 24K Life Code*. The real question is, what and who do you believe in?

Sometimes it takes the power of just one amazing feat or person to open your belief within. Have you heard the story of Roger Bannister? It is a well-known story, but I'm going to give you the CliffsNotes version anyway. Roger Bannister was a British middle-distance athlete and neurologist who ran the first sub-four-minute mile in history. Breaking the four-minute mile was considered a human impossibility before Roger achieved it. He set his mind to break through four minutes, and he did it. Since he broke the record, thousands have followed suit, including high school teenage athletes. The moral to this story is that nothing you desire is impossible if you believe and set your actions in motion.

Roger Bannister, Jim Carrey, Steve Jobs . . . all of these ordinary humans have done incredible things that had never been thought possible. If you read their stories, you can see they all lived by a personal belief code that they refused to deny. Their belief in themselves led to astronomical success in their respective fields. It is imperative to have your own belief code. A personal belief code is crucial to living a 24K Life. Belief and understanding yourself are critical to self-mastery, living your best life, and leaving nothing to chance. The energy, confidence, and power that resides in personal belief has conquered nations and changed the world time and time again.

Adolph Hitler, the German politician and leader of the Nazi party, had an erroneous belief so strong that he rallied a nation to adopt his position and pushed the world into war. In another example, the belief of one holy man created Christianity, which became one of the most significant religions in history. Whether you are a Christian or not is irrelevant; the story alone has manifested billions of global believers for over two thousand years.

Your internal beliefs are personal truths buried deep inside you. Your morals, values, ethics, politics, religion, and view on yourself were all developed before your tenth birthday. When you consider the origination of your beliefs or truths, they most likely came from your parents, extended family, and the surrounding community. Your mom and dad gave you their beliefs as they experienced and saw them. Many of those inherited beliefs are likely very useful and accurate. Some of our learned beliefs may be considered dysfunctional, and those are the ones we need to rewire in our mindset.

Early in life, I was often asked if I was a football or basketball player. As a big kid, I'm sure most people thought it was a natural question to ask. Subsequently, it influenced my decision to play a sport even though I had little understanding of sports at age eight. I clearly remember asking over and over why football players took the ball and jumped on each other every time they said hut one, hut two. It just didn't make any sense to me. A guy would be reeling in pain and then carried off on a stretcher never to be seen again. And why were they all so dirty all of the time? Despite having such a little understanding, my belief and vision of myself had been established. Everyone basically told me or insinuated that I should be an athlete, so football eventually became a significant part of my life.

Through my success in sports, I received local and regional accolades for my on-field and court accomplishments. Sports delivered attention, trophies, rings, letterman jackets, and sweaters, all of the things most people dream they could have. This started because of a belief that was thrust upon me at an early age.

I find it intriguing that no one asked me what subject I liked to study or if I was a good student. Imagine if the majority of adults who met me had inquired and discussed the amazing things in the ocean or asked me what I thought about the constellations? What if someone told me how cool it would be to become a doctor?

Don't worry; it's never too late to unwind the foundational distortions that are impacting your ability to succeed. Rewiring your mindset and beliefs will take a lot of work to discover and undo, but you can do it. Many of us believe we are doing great and that there is no reason we need to reinvent ourselves or our beliefs. You may not need a complete makeover; maybe you just need a deep dive into what limiting beliefs are in your operating system.

Like me, maybe you currently do things because of expectations or pressures that were put on you as a child. Most children assume whatever adults say is gospel. Once you identify what you need to restructure, search your mind and actions at every single step to become a better version of yourself.

ACCEPT AND STAND IN YOUR TRUTH

The first rule of belief is to never lie to yourself. I don't think you should lie to anyone, but it is a definite deal breaker to lie to yourself.

Knowing who you are and standing in your truth sounds so easy to do: this is who I am, and this is what I believe and everyone will simply accept it. The problem is we are programmed to be concerned with what others think about us. We say internally, I know what I believe, but I'm concerned about what others believe about what I believe so I will adjust.

If we're being totally honest, our status and conceived position in society and our inner circles are what drive most of the decisions we make. The entire social media phenomena is so powerful because of the importance we place on what others think and believe. How many selfies do you take before selecting the one that is acceptable to share with the world? How many times did you check to see how many people liked your latest post and commented about how great you are? The notification ding has replaced Pavlov's bell, and the endorphins rush undeniable.

"Because one believes in oneself, one doesn't try to convince others. Because one is content with oneself, one doesn't need other's approval. Because one accepts oneself, the whole world accepts him or her."

Lao Tzu

To stand in your truth and on your beliefs, you have to find out which of your core beliefs need to be reframed and regenerate them into a more pure version of who you desire to be.

PROTECTING THE MACHINE

Every family has a producer. A producer is the one who does the laundry, the cooking, the taxi driving, the bill paying. The producer, in many cases, completes close to 80 percent of the work and receives 20 percent of the credit. This is not an uncommon phenomenon. It's called the Pareto Principle.

The Pareto Principle (also known as the 80/20 rule, the law of the vital few, or the principle of factor sparsity) states that, for many events, roughly 80 percent of the effects come from 20 percent of the causes.[10] The principle is named after Italian economist Vilfredo Pareto, who noted the 80/20 connection while at the University of Lausanne in 1896, as published in his first work, Cours d'économie politique. Mostly, Pareto's research showed that approximately 80 percent of the land in Italy was owned by 20 percent of the population. His research also showed that only 20 percent of the crops produced from the land was suitable for consumption. It is an axiom of business management that "80 percent of sales come from 20 percent of clients."

If you are the producer in your family or business, you are going to have to work extra hard to protect your mind, body, and soul. How many of your basic needs do you make sure you are getting daily? Water, food, physical activity, rest, and a quiet moment all to yourself are required for proper health.

Each of us needs six to eight hours of sleep a day.[11] It has been studied and proven that longevity of life goes hand in hand with adequate rest. So many people operate on four or five hours of sleep and are technically breaking down the machine. You are the machine. The machine refers to your total being that tirelessly pushes to deliver the results you set out to accomplish. We aren't built to last on minimal recovery. The body and the mind need rest because it is the most important machine in the universe. Take care of it.

Ignore Outside Noise

We live in an exceptionally noisy age, and our thoughts and feelings are drowned out by noise. Have you ever noticed how much you don't pay attention to your thoughts and feelings? Most thoughts are flushed out by the opinions of others or our perception of how others may view our decisions. It's interesting that people will take a poll on social media asking for input on making a personal decision. Have people honestly forgotten how to make their own choices? Success is an inside job, and you should never forget that you're the master creator.

Our ability to think has been circumvented and disabled with so many tools and distractions. Don't remember where the keys are? Hey, push this button on your phone and those keys will start beeping. Don't remember what you needed from the store? Here is a picture of what's not in the refrigerator your spouse sent to your phone.

Noise can come from a variety of places:

- Radio
- Social media
- Television
- Video games

- Mobile phones

- Parties

- People

Protecting yourself from noise is real work. Our lives are bombarded with ads subliminally pushing us to buy now and inciting us with FOMO (fear of missing out). We allow ourselves to be guilted into trying to keep up with the Joneses and the Smiths.

Be unwavering in your stand to protect your thoughts. It's tough, but you are getting stronger every time you take a stand and fight the noise. The mind is like a muscle. Build your mind to be strong, fearless, unwavering, and focused.

BELIEVE 50 PERCENT

Building the mind includes meditation, journaling, and making a decision. Sometimes making a decision can mean seeking counsel, which could be a wise thing to do. But understand that someone else's advice is not more important than your own thoughts. We are a culmination of our interactions and experiences. When we process a decision, we pull from our historical references and results. When you get advice, the advisor is drawing from their historical references and results. I have a rule about advice: believe 50 percent of what people tell you.

How many times have you complained that you don't have time to work out or complete a task on your to-do list? Maybe you plan to meditate, make a grocery list, or replace the tires on your car but can't seem to get to it. The reality is that if you track your time, you will discover you have plenty of time to do it all. You chose to do something else. Others do the same thing. They say they go to the gym, read several books a month, and never miss a meeting, but this is their projection of who they wish to be. The reality is that results don't lie. What people say they do and what they actually get accomplished is often at opposition. This is why you should only follow the advice of those who are living the answers you seek. You can identify the successful ones not by what they say, but what they consistently do.

Growing up in church, our beloved pastor would occasionally deliver a sermon that dealt with problems in the workplace or with topics he never personally experienced. He was a child prodigy and became an ordained minister at the very early age of twelve. He was the most amazing man I ever met, exceptionally anointed. However, I always wondered how to take advice from his sermons when I knew he never dealt with an issue personally. Maybe he was gifted with insight that I had dismissed, but I have always struggled with taking counsel from someone if they haven't been where I want to go.

Unfortunately, I have learned the hard way that most people have good intentions but often only tell half the story. Either they are uninformed, inexperienced, or exaggerating. When seeking advice, listen to the entire message, but only apply the advice that resonates in your heart. Throw the rest of the information away. You don't want useless information messing up your mind.

DON'T ACCEPT OR ADOPT MEDIOCRITY

You should never accept or adopt mediocrity. Remember, you don't have to keep the limiting story you have been telling yourself for years. We all have incredible unlimited potential, but we don't operate from there. We operate or perform at our expectations and belief levels. Period! But every time you accomplish something new, you reset your baseline to a higher level.

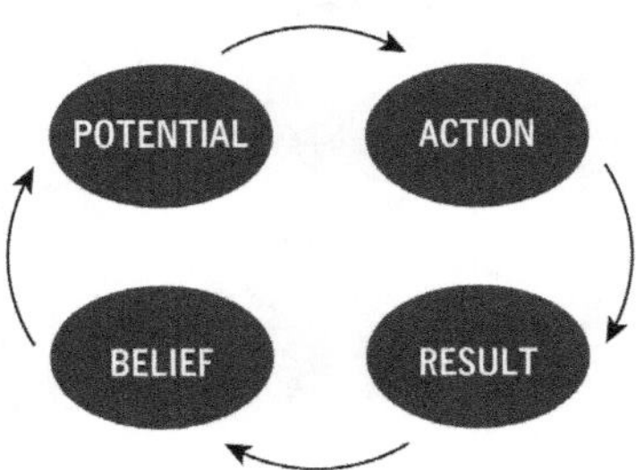

The diagram[12] shows the flow of our beliefs related to our personal performance results. At the top are our beliefs and expectations. We take action based on what we believe and expect from ourselves (past performances). We then get the results of our actions, which reinforce the original belief, and reinforced belief, helps us see our higher potential. The process keeps repeating itself.

Greater action produces greater results, which enforce your beliefs and expectations. This all results in a higher expression of your potential! This is a huge concept to understand, so I hope you get the clarity of the principle. Remember what happened to Roger Bannister? It took a sense of extreme belief and certainty for him to do what was considered impossible. He was able to create confidence in his mind without seeing any proof anywhere in the world that it could be done. Roger Bannister's amazing feat didn't happen with magic. Each and everyone of us has the ability to dig deep within and pull out our personal amazing. We just have to decide to be our best and let nothing stand in our way.

"To be yourself in a world that is constantly trying to make you some-thing else is the greatest accomplishment."
Ralph Waldo Emerson

When you become sure of something, when every part of your makeup believes it because you focus on it every single day, something happens. You begin to pay special attention to things that help you achieve what you're after, things you otherwise never would have noticed. It is imperative to adopt a belief code, a 24K Life Code, that consistently challenges and raises your belief level.

CHAPTER 5
STRONGER THAN KRYPTONITE

There is a running theme in your life that has held you back from growing and prospering into your best life. You are good-looking, smart, communicate well, have a solid sense of what's right and wrong, and you never shy away from hard work, so what's missing? Why are you still running in circles? You keep asking yourself, "Why can't I get ahead?" These are all questions we ask ourselves and rarely can answer. One answer that slapped me in the face after asking myself this question was, "You're always thinking about or trying to build a better mousetrap."

Having a better mousetrap means that while I love the idea I'm working on, the bright new idea I suddenly thought of is so much better. I want to drop what I'm was doing and start that new thing right away! Why waste another second on what I was doing when there is a much better plan ahead? This is definitely a kryptonite obstacle.

Kryptonite is the reference I use to describe obstacles or things that are holding me back. Kryptonite weakens my ability to have the machine operating at optimal production.

Imagine being an author writing books for sale, but they never get sold because most of them are only 75 percent complete. Stupid, right? Yes, it's idiotic. The question is, why did the books never get finished? It could be because not enough research was done or you don't like the endings. Some hidden but obvious reason has kept you from successfully moving forward. This blockage is what professionals call a scotoma. A scotoma is a blind spot in our heads. Something that is relatively obvious holding us back from accomplishing a plan, freezing us in place, but we can't see it or recognize it. Our scotomas are kryptonite.

Other than the better mousetrap, another scotoma of mine was that I loved the big picture but hated the details. In sports I just wanted to play the game. But playing the game is the reward, the prize, the showcase. The practice field is where excellence is born.

I didn't realize that what I was saying and asking for was in direct opposition to what I was doing. I worked hard but only at the big stuff. It wasn't until I took radical ownership of where I was and realized I was falling short on the details that things started to turn around in my favor.

Some of the most dangerous types of kryptonite or obstacles that can block your success are:

- Limiting beliefs
- Distractions
- Fear of success or failure
- Procrastination

If you have one or a multiple of these issues, you have to identify them, own up to them, and eliminate them. Make your weakness your bitch by focusing on it and eliminating it. You can't run from it because it's not going away.

There are experts outside of your circle equipped to help people get over their issues and move their lives forward. If you are so prideful that you can't get help, stop reading, because this isn't the book for you. Everyone, including the best of the best, has mentors, coaches, or advisors who help them become successful. I used to believe that I was enough and that I didn't need anyone's help, but I was 100 percent wrong. It's not common for men to admit when they need help. It's even more uncommon for a man actually to go and get some help. But it's imperative that you do so if you want to be your best self.

In 2008, all the clouds in my world had turned gray and were accumulating in my head. My business was suffering from the market collapse, my kids were struggling in school, my wife and I weren't on the same page or in the same book. I felt like the world's biggest loser. Things were so obviously a mess for me that a friend made a suggestion.

Friend: "Hey, why don't you go and talk to a professional therapist?"

Me: "Black men don't go to therapy."

Friend: "Why not?"

Me: "We just don't."

Of course, being a type-A person and an expert problem solver, this was a big issue blocking my progress. I began seeing therapy signs, billboards, TV commercials, and newspaper ads for stress therapy everywhere I went. I started to think about it more and more until a fantastic thought popped in my head: I know a therapist whom I love like a mother. It was incredible how blind I had been not to think of this person all along.

One of the main reasons I rejected the thought of therapy was because I was worried I wouldn't be able to find someone I could trust to know me and help me while not judging me. Problem solved! There was someone available to help and it hadn't even occurred to me. This amazing woman, Dr. Harshman, was the mother of a fellow high school football player and I remembered she had thought the world of me. I hadn't seen her in well over ten years, but I knew she would remember me.

She agreed to see me, we met and talked, and she did what no one else had done for me up until that point in my life: she saw me. She saw me as a person, not as a husband, a son, a father, an athlete, an advisor, or a church deacon. She saw me. After three or four sessions, I was back to full alpha mode, and I owe the change to being shown how to take radical responsibility for myself and only myself.

"Everyone thinks of changing the world,
but no one thinks of changing himself."
Leo Tolstoy

Excuses We Make

"If only" is a common phrase people use. If only I were taller, smarter, better looking, or luckier, I would have the world in the palm of my hands. If only my wife would support me, encourage me, or love me more, I could accomplish a wonderful life. A common one I hear is, "I will be ready once my kids are older." No matter which way you look at it, all of these statements represent someone making excuses for not going after what they are called to do in life.

There will never be an exact time or a perfect way to take the actions necessary to move your life forward. If you look for an excuse, your creative subconscious will find one. You are always fighting yourself to stay the same, not to improve. Once you realize who the real enemy is—you—maybe you will take the appropriate action to crush your fears and hang-ups and move on.

I learned many years ago that excuses are useless, and unless you take radical ownership for yourself, you will always be able to find an excuse. It takes one decision at a time to get the results you desire. We make decisions all day long, and if you make excuses that allow you to remain the same, you will most certainly remain the same. New decisions result in a new direct.

IT CAN'T WAIT

If you take a poll and ask strangers what single thing interferes the most with their success, you will hear the word procrastination. Procrastination is the ultimate kryptonite. Google how to stop procrastinating, and you will get countless lists of the top ten things to do to avoid procrastination.

I've been a secret ops top agent of procrastination. I'm a bit weird. I can go all out on something I am interested in. I will sleep for four hours and get up and get right back at my objective. If it's losing weight, I will myopically focus on every spoon or fork full of food, monitor every calorie consumed, burned, or wasted. My scale batteries might burn out, or my spreadsheet may have to be added to my phone documents reader, but I am all in. Yes, I am very aggressive at what I'm interested in. A full-out, relentless beast. The procrastination problem comes into play with all of the things I put aside when I am hyper-focused on that one thing.

Through the process of building a personal code, I learned it is very dangerous to only focus on the actions that will get you to your results. Dismissing things like people, assignments, and tasks will create new problems that you will soon have to tackle. When you let things go for another day, you soon realize a day can turn into a week and a week into a month.

We all have things we prefer to do and things we wish we never had to do. When it comes to overcoming the universal roadblock, it is best to put those things you normally put off on your schedule as a dedicated task. That way no matter what happens, if you honor your schedule, everything will eventually get handled.

THE SELF-PRESERVATION QUESTION

Every obstacle has a solution, but you have to be willing to do whatever it takes to overcome it.

Some obstacles require asking a self-preservation question. When facing a problem or obstacle, you have to ask yourself if this is something you can do something about. Can you control this kryptonite? Once this question is asked and answered, you have a distinctive path to move forward. Immediately begin to design and implement the appropriate solution.

If you can't do anything, the objective is to not worry about it. This particular problem is not within your wheelhouse to fix. Most of the time, if something is out of our control, it rarely affects us the way we imagine it would. We worry in monster-size motion pictures while things happen in pocket-size snapshots, if they happen at all.

If the answer to the self-preservation question is "Yes, I can do something about this," then it's time to roll up your sleeves and map a strategy to overcome yourself. Your life's opponent is a formative adversary and loves you very much.

REPLACING BAD BELIEFS

The kryptonite that is always with you is your limiting beliefs. Limiting beliefs are being delivered to you every day at every opportunity. They come to you through that little voice in your head telling you why you can't, shouldn't, or won't get to the next level.

Decide to change the words you use and the things you say to yourself immediately. That still, small voice isn't going anywhere anytime soon. This makes it imperative to hear it, recognize it, and change it. Create a positive tone, a consistent temperament, and a daily word choice that empowers your mind and your heart.

The best way to create impacting change is to grab a pad and paper, ideally a personal journal, and track all of the negative, self-deprecating words you say about yourself. For me, I only said negative things when something didn't go my way. Maybe I left my office for a meeting and forgot my car keys on my desk. I would get to the car and search every pocket and crevice, most likely twice, as if the keys could magically pop into my coat pocket the third time I checked. During the entire walk to retrieve my keys and all of the way back I would chastise myself for being stupid, forgetful, and always wasting time.

The first thing I changed once I realized I was self-sabotaging was to note every negative thought I had and every curse word I said about myself. I was shocked at how many times I berated myself. I began forcing myself to stop mid-thought and halt the assault. Once I did this, I began to laugh, as I could now see the negativity coming every time I stubbed my toe or forgot my keys.

Once I was aware of my thoughts and stopped them, I needed to replace the negative words with more positive ones. I began to say things like, "This is strange, I never forget my keys. I am always making great decisions, so this must be that one time in a million I made a bad choice." It may take a while to rewire those thoughts, but it will be mighty powerful when you do.

AFRAID TO GO ALL IN

"I've got a theory that if you give 100% all of the time,
things will work out in the end."
Larry Bird

Everyone knows that fear is kryptonite, and most of the time results in destructive paralysis. We have all been scared to act. At times we only act out of an extreme fight or flight response. The tricky kryptonite is the fear of success. I can give you details about the first-hand experience I had with this.

In my college football days, I just wanted to get to game day and show my stuff. But once I realized I had to show my excellence during practice to get on the field on game day, I had a new problem. In my pea brain, if I went all out during the core practice, I would not have enough gas to complete conditioning at the end of practice. I feared I would run out of energy, pass out due to exhaustion, and the coach would call me out as a slacker. My perception was that I would not only fail but do so in a catastrophic way and in front of the entire team and staff of coaches. Remember the movie Carrie? "They're all going to laugh at me" was ringing in my head.

My idiotic solution was to give 90 percent effort during practice but save the last 10 percent for wind sprints and fifty-yard gassers at the end. I thought it was reasonable.

It turns out that this whole thought process was wrong. What coaches knew, the other players knew, and what I should have figured out was that being fast at the end when the team stars had kicked ass all day was not going to win me any extra points. What I needed was a new mindset. I needed to understand that the fear of giving my all could keep me from getting what I wanted. In life, what many people fear is giving 100 percent and still not meeting the mark. I clearly remember thinking, What if I give my all and come up short? I'll be devastated. I will be a loser, a nobody, another busted high school superstar. The reality is we only have our time right now to bring and deliver our best selves. Every day it is our insights and experiences that makes us better, and we no longer need to be afraid to give our all. As I move through the day, I give all I have and know that when I have more, I will deliver that too.

Kryptonite is not devastating unless you lie down and let it control your life. Whatever is holding you back, standing in your way, or creating stress, reach out and grab it, shake it, and take aggressive actions to conquer it as soon as possible. Recognizing your obstacles and deciding how to attack them or if you should attack them is essential. The truth is that problems don't going away on their own, and you have to overcome them to get to the mountain top.

CHAPTER 6
LIVING YOUR BEST LIFE

Living your best life is your choice. Most people don't see it this way because of their view. Perspective is everything, especially when you consider your overall outlook on life. The way you see life dictates the way you look at yourself and others when measuring your possible outcomes or successes. Operating and making daily decisions based on a proper perspective can mean the difference between a $100 contract and a $100,000 contract.

When trying to assess your view on how you see things, ask yourself, "What is my macro view of life?" Some people consider life a box of chocolates or a bowl of cherries. I've heard people say life is a . . .

- Gift
- Journey
- Game
- Challenge
- Mountain railroad
- Test
- Race

Starting to get the picture of how many perspectives could exist? We are all very different and have opinions based on our upbringing, beliefs, and experiences. We can't avoid being influenced by these things because they have made us who we are up until this very moment. Understanding this is vital because opinions, beliefs, and experiences are the basis in which we each choose to face the world. Consider that two co-workers have a career-changing project they must complete together to win a new account. One worker sees life as a gift while the other sees life as a challenge. Each can only approach the project as they are.

The gift worker is honored to be able to work on the project and will do everything to return the giver's grace with an even better gift. The challenge worker starts right out of the gate considering everything that will interfere with the successful completion of the project. Focusing on the negative aspects possibly draws more negative aspects. These approaches will follow the two people through the course of the project. While the two see things from completely different perspectives, they can produce the results if they divide the work properly and honor each other's position.

I am not suggesting that you need or must operate from a specific view or approach. I am suggesting that you know what your view of life is and make certain you flush out the flaws that hinder you from living your best life.

I always viewed life as a game, and all games must be won or lost. This perspective, like most, has its advantages and disadvantages. For me, the benefits are that it's just a game and games can be played over and over. Most games also have rules, which means everyone has a chance to win based on their contribution and skills.

I remember how my view of life as a game negatively exploded and caused me to make a life-changing decision. I was working for a large securities firm and made a decision to switch from commission-based revenue to a fee-based revenue. I was the first to do this in our firm, so everything related to the business was new. At that time with the firm, once you exceeded a certain production level, you received an annual bonus, and no day was better than a bonus day. Bonuses were handed out once a year in the spring, so it was a great way to usher in the summer season.

Like every other representative in the office, I carefully tracked my commission and bonus numbers monthly. One year on bonus day I expected to get a $35,000 check, but to my surprise, it was only $15,000. I opened the envelope, and after I took several deep breaths, I steeled my nerves and decided it must have been a simple oversight that would easily be fixed. Rules are rules, and the bonus schedule was clearly laid out, so I just needed to get this fixed.

The following Monday I approached the securities manager and laid out my position and understanding of the bonus rules. He explained the company had to decide to devalue the fee-based business as "not as profitable" as other business, so my bonus was appropriately calculated. I had done well over the volume required to equal the commission bonus numbers, so this made no sense to me, and I made that clear in no uncertain terms.

The flaw in my position was that I looked at life and business as a game, and I erroneously expected the coach I played for to be fair. Life isn't fair, and if I had been paying attention, I would have seen this coming. I let my perspective influence my ability to live my best life and was miserable until I took ownership and adjusted my view.

I still look at life as a game; I just added some addendums to my approach. My first new addendum is to consider everyone's perspective that I'm playing with. Upon review, I plan out how we can all win based on our specific needs and perspectives on life. I also do my best to be prepared for the outliers and how new interactions or players will play into whatever role or game we are trying to win. Adjusting my view has allowed me to stay on track more often and definitely live life closer to my golden plan.

Your Best Life Is Past, Present, and Future

You have several choices when it comes to what timeframe you will focus on in order to live your best life.

Living in the past. The people I know who live in the past are constantly replaying the highlights of their history. They recant how great or poor their high school life was and why it was that way. They compare what is happening now to what happened in the past. The present reality is lived in comparison to the past. Most things are judged on the past, and it is very hard for them to truly be present or envision the future.

Living in the present. There is no better moment than the present. Living in the moment is a strong way to stay clear and connected with reality. People who live in the moment are a bit more at ease because they are not thinking about what could go right or wrong in the future. By being present, they are not thinking in great detail about how things went in the past. More people should live in the moment because there is tremendous power in having current clarity.

"Peak experiences as rare, exciting, oceanic, deeply moving, exhilarating, elevating experiences that generate an advanced form of perceiving reality, and are even mystic and magical in their effect upon the experimenter."
Abraham Maslow

Living in the future. Only living in the future is just as tough as only living in the past. When you're focused on what is to come, you discount any lessons learned in the past. Living in the future means you may actually miss an amazing present opportunity to enjoy life right now.

The challenge to living your best life is to be able to decipher your own view of how best to draw on the past for lessons, the present for reality, and the future for possibilities. Analyze how you use the three to define people, places, things, and events. If you find that your opinion jades how you move and interact, you should begin to adjust and improve your position and thoughts. Too much focus on any one is most likely unhealthy or unproductive. Think about having a well-thought-out view and understanding of how your beliefs, experiences, and mindset fit into your life. Once you have decided, master the thoughts, feelings, and actions that direct your path and you will be on your way to living a golden life.

BATTLES AND WARS

Life has so many truths and beliefs, some based on timeframes and some on perspectives. As we work, live, and play with others, a decision on what truths and beliefs are imperative to fight and uphold becomes essential. Some matters are worth a battle, and some are worth a war, while others deserve little to no attention at all. I contend most matters should be passed on all together.

Most people don't distinguish between what is insignificant, a battle, or a war; therefore, they remain poised to fight at all times. The better you get at self-mastery, the more discerning you will become on what is helpful, relevant, and important. When you are unclear about what is important, everything seems to be essential, and your natural instinct is to fight to hold on for dear life. When you are in the dark, you can't clearly see what is there and if what's there is good or bad.

Deciding if you are in a battle or a war is easy when you understand your foundational beliefs and core values. You should never give in or turn away from your core beliefs because they are the summation of who you are now and who you may become in the future. Therefore, in tough times or times of controversy, the first question you should ask is, "Is this something that will matter in a day, a month, a year?" Another way to put it is, "Will this go against my soul or my beliefs?" If your answer is no, why fight at all? Do you want to be known as the one who fights at every turn or the one who seeks a higher resolution as often as possible?

When I was playing college football, I engaged a most unfortunate ill-timed battle I thought was a war. It was a scorching hot August day, and we were completing practice for the day. At the end of the second practice, we had what was called conditioning. It was always brutal. This particular day the coach said, "We're are going to run sideline to sideline three-quarter speed over and back for four sets." This was music to a receivers' ears because we could run sprints all day.

The whistle blew for the last set, and we all took off over to one sideline and back to the starting spot. Tired, hot, and sweaty, the only question was, "When's dinner?" But then the coach said, "Do it again. Gant didn't run." As the fastest tight end, I had decided all I had to do was come in first so I boastfully yelled, "Hey, Coach. You said three-quarter speed and I came in first." He, of course, said, "Shut up," and everyone had to run again.

As you can imagine, there were a hundred hot, sweaty, and now pissed-off cavemen. Begrudgingly we all ran back and again I came in first. Perfect, right? Wrong. Coach said, "Gant didn't run. Do it again." At this point I was getting punched in the back of the helmet and cursed at by my loving teammates. Of course this meant war. I again yelled, "Hey, Coach, I came in first by far this time," and he repeated, "Shut up," and everyone ran again.

I unleashed a tirade of expletives and abuses, including telling him he had a Napoleon complex and that everyone, even the assistant coaches, hated him. Needless to say, this did not end in my favor. In my defense, I was not a self-master and just a twenty-year-old kid desperate to please everyone, so having a hundred guys pissed at me distorted my view. I wasn't even close to understanding how to pick my battles, let alone determine if it was a battle at all.

In hindsight it wasn't a war or a battle; it was just mind games, and I lost big-time. I have replayed the experience over the past years and used it as a monumental moment in my personal development. The lesson, however, has paid golden dividends for many years ever since. This experience was my fast track to learning the difference between battles and wars.

"Sometimes by losing a battle, you find a way to win the war."
Confucius

Today I am willing to not fight at all or lose a battle if that's what it takes to win the war. Wars are things that go against my core values or my beliefs. Wars are life-or-death scenarios, and I don't intend to die. When you go to war, be willing to cut ties with the closest constituents you have. Severing relations may include business partners, spouses, or even parents. This is why you should be very reluctant to go to war. War is a bloody undertaking that most likely will result in a severe alteration in the path of your destiny. Be slow to anger and quick to forgive. Consider your battles as opportunities to help others win or, even better, a way for everyone to win. The win may not be considered epic, but when all parties walk away a bit satisfied, everyone lives to play another day.

CONSISTENT WINS

As young children, we were always told to be kind. No matter what the contest or circumstance, it was drilled in us to be helpful, share, and under no circumstances rub your win in another's face. Even today it is considered good sportsmanship to meet your opponent after a game and tell them, "Good game," win or lose. I think it's the most absurd thing ever to say that. Seems like we should say, "You lost, you loosing loser. Better luck never!" I jest, and I understand it's good sportsmanship, but do you really want to hear the guy or gal who just beat you sincerely say, "Great job"? Imagine losing a promotion to a coworker. Are you going to say, "Hey, Martha, I'm so happy for you, you really deserved that position more than I did"? I'm sure there are a few who would say that and mean it. But most wouldn't. I wouldn't have been that supportive in the past. Today, I realize through taking radical ownership that not getting a promotion has more to do with me than anything outside of me.

These days when little kids compete, there is no winner or loser because no score is recorded, and everyone gets to play equally. This is fantastic grooming for what real life is like; don't you agree? Not even close. As an adult, no referee or parent committee checks on the equality of life. The reason there is such a massive disparity in wealth is that the wealthy unapologetically look out for their best interests first, second, and third. There is no "we all win" in their master plan. The wealthy aren't wrong; everyone else is wrong.

Good schools don't tell smart kids to dumb it down and learn to be nice or wait for the less intelligent kids to catch up. They put those kids in advanced classes, separating the best from the rest whenever possible. The nature of winning is that the strong survive and thrive while the weak support, care for, and nurture the elite few. The prevailing perception is that there is not enough winning to go around, so depending on your faction, either you're told to share the victories or told you can win next time if you keep trying.

> *"Consistent small wins make you a big winner over time."*
> Derick Gant

The best way to enjoy the spoils is to be victorious. Take every opportunity to be your best, bring your best, and leave nothing to chance. When you deliver the goods, you win. Create a mindset that holds the idea that a win is a win, large or small. Developing this mindset is the path to creating the habit and belief that you are a winner. Once you believe it, good things will continue unfolding for you daily. Remember that like attracts like, and as you win, your creative subconscious is looking for more ways to make those wins happen automatically.

GLITTER LIKE GOLD

Life is your golden nugget, your priceless asset that you get to barter and trade with. Consider life as your opportunity to create anything you wish, but you must make the wish or you will waste the opportunity. The beauty of life is that we are all amazingly and uniquely made. We all have one-of-a-kind fingerprints, facial features, and eyes. In the history of the world, there has never been any two souls who were exactly alike. That thought alone should solidify the fact that you get to be you 100 percent and no one can do you better than you.

It is your duty, your obligation, to be the best you possible. Why would you consciously decide to live a life half or a third of what is meant for you? I want all of my life. We all know that life can be hard at times, but what if we could make it less so? Self-mastery is a unique key to less stress and fewer hard times. Understanding your perspective and mastering you and the way you act with yourself and interact with others is amazingly powerful.

There is no shortcut to understanding the depths of who you are inside and why you react to things on the outside. Each of us has to do our personal soul searching. We must test our faith, beliefs, and understanding to ascertain the path we are to follow to live our best life and to reach our destination healthy, wealthy, and happy.

It is never too late to gain a clear understanding of who you are and how you operate. The outside pressure to conform is what makes us think we are not up to spreading our wings. No matter what is said or done to taint your outlook, it is within your power to decide to overcome any obstacle and be great. People love a winner. If you have lost over and over and over again, keep fighting. Be the Rocky Balboa of your life and decide you are a champion within. You may not appear to a champion to the general public, but as you keep working, fighting, and creating every day, the results will eventually show you as a champion.

*"Don't give in to excuses that can keep you
from really living the best life God has for you."*
Joyce Meyers

Age is not a factor, and education is not an excuse. Access to any- and everything you need to know is available within minutes if you decide to search for it. The desire to be your best and your understanding of your real value are the keys to your power. Hold your standards high, yourself accountable, and demand self-discipline if you want others to see the excellence you bring the world.

PART II
GOLD MATTERS

CHAPTER 7
MILLIONAIRE MINDSET

The 24K Life is not about being rich. However, we all need money to survive and thrive. Most people operate off of a monetary survival instinct. People believe in scarcity, that there isn't enough money to go around. They have decided it's better to grab what they can as fast as they can because if they don't, someone else will consume their portion. Because of this prevailing mindset, people willingly trade time for money.

We all have the same twenty-four hours a day. When you trade your time for money, you automatically place a cap on the amount of money you can make regardless of your value. Punching a clock puts food on the table, but you better show up to work today if you want to eat tomorrow. Let's be crystal clear, there is nothing wrong with punching a clock. It's just that I'd prefer it be your choice not your mandate.

"If everyone has the same number of hours in the day, why do some people seem to get so much more done than others? How do they do more, achieve more, earn more, have more? If time is the currency of achievement, then why are some able to cash in their allotment for more chips than others?

The answer is they make getting to the heart of things the heart of their approach. They go small. Going small is ignoring all the things you could do and doing what you should do. It's recognizing that not all things matter equally and finding the things that matter most. It's a tighter way to connect what you do with what you want. It's realizing that extraordinary results are directly determined by how narrow you can make your focus."[13]

Gary Keller

When it comes to basic money mindsets, there are two kinds that resonate deeply from my experience: owners and renters. An owner's mindset is one that understands it's best to possess the clock that renters are punching every day. Owners are exceptionally aware of the value workers bring to their organizations and they expect a hefty return on the paycheck they provide.

Have you ever thought about how much company revenue someone must generate to earn a paycheck? Based on 2013 earnings figures,11 the two most efficient companies, Google and Facebook, generate $1 million of revenue per employee per year, while the average Salaries at Google, Inc. range from an average of $65,595 to $162,430 a year.[14]

In an average company, the average revenue per employee is about $190k to $210k per year compared with the average income of $50,000. The disparity between what the owners make in revenue and what the renter receives in compensation is a lot more clear. Consider how a professional sports team owner commits to pay one player $100 million over a six-year period. The owner has to be creating an astronomical amount of revenue above and beyond all of the player contracts to run the franchise and still make a substantial profit.

If you want to transform your financial life, consider establishing an owner's mindset. To begin to build this, identify what you can control or own and how you can begin to keep more of the

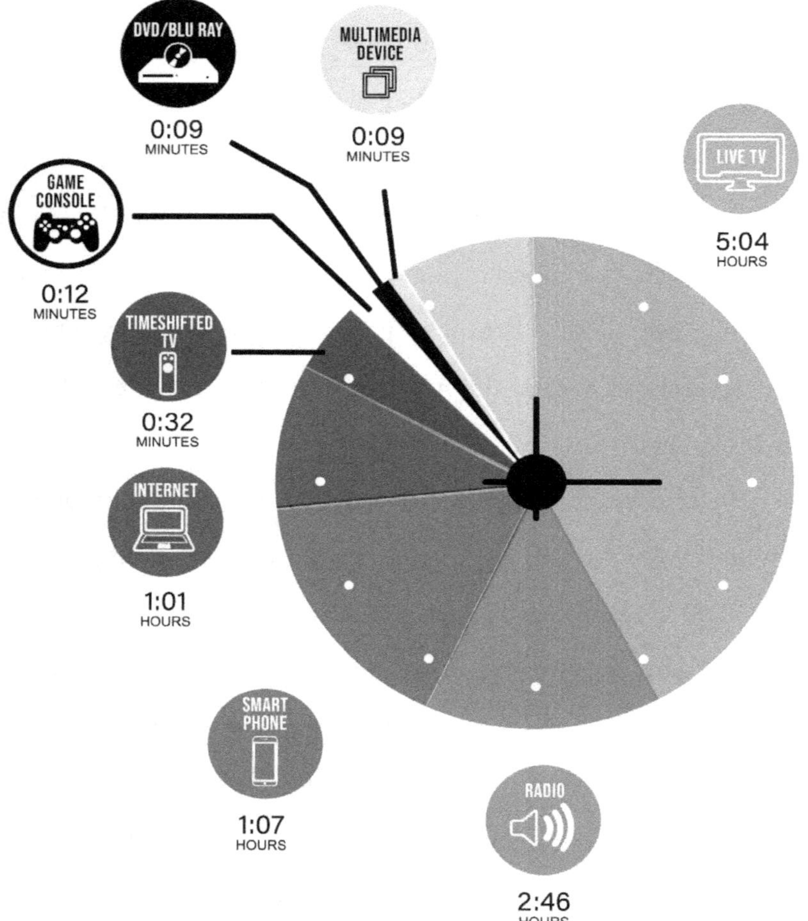

money you earn. In addition to that, determine how you can get your reserves working to make you money while you sleep. One thing we can all do is start the process of controlling our after work personal hours.

It's interesting how many hours of the day people are playing with their phone, iPad, and computer, or watching TV. People have found an escape, something to occupy their mind. And that phone or distraction is begging them to spend more and more money they don't have. Today you can sit in your living room and have groceries, dog food, or a dress delivered to your door with a few taps on your mobile device. All of these are traps to get into your pocket and keep you broke with a renters mindset.[15]

Every dollar in circulation has a duty to fulfill, and either you assign your dollars a responsibility to improve your life or someone else will use it to improve theirs.

YOUR MONEY YOUR MOVE

It's my duty to show you how to break the cycle of mediocrity and move your mind, body, and wallet into abundance. Prosperity takes a vision that is greater than immediate gratification. It is also my duty to let you know that having a renter's or a scarcity mindset is not all your fault. A scarcity mindset has deep roots that were developed in our psyche from the times when we had to fight nature for food, water, and shelter. But now our economic system has taken this old programming and weaponized it against the consumer. Material goods and services are displayed as a constant reminder of what we don't have. This keeps us focused and distracted on what is happening outside of our lives in lieu of the real important things going on inside of our lives.

One day I was visiting a friend and mentor of mine. He was heading into a meeting and invited me to sit in and observe their corporate marketing team. I wanted to see what was behind the magic curtain of success, and what I learned in that hour was mind-blowing.

My dear friend owns and operates hundreds of gas stations covering four or five states. We're talking big business. Well, as a loyal friend, I only buy gas from his shops because friends support friends and I need gas anyway so why not hook up my boy. Well, I thought I was hooking him up, but this day as I sat in on this meeting, I was the one who got the hook-up, and now I'm sharing my hook-up with you. Because that's what friends do!

I learned that the gas station has two main objectives, and buying gas isn't one of them. What? Yes, I said it right. The station isn't concerned with you purchasing gas. They know you are going to do that because you need it. Their concern is getting you into the store while you fill up your vehicle.

To get you to come in, they understand your natural state of laziness. You have a need, one that you should go to the grocery store to fill, but hey, you're already here at the station, so you think, I bet they have light bulbs just the size I need. Yup, third isle, middle to the left. These bulbs are available, but they will cost more because the station can't buy them in a competitive bulk size.

Now that you are in the store, the real objective is getting you to purchase a fountain drink. I know you think I'm nuts, but let's look at the math. A 14-ounce coffee costs the company $.04 and sells for $.89, a 16-ounce costs $.04 and sells for $.99, and finally a 20-ounce costs $.04 and sells for $1.09. Can you see all that profit?

This particular marketing meeting was engaged in intense dialogue to determine which brand of beer should be showcased in the beer cave. A major portion of the discussion was focused on what specific height and position certain beers should be placed. The information and detail presented were stunning.

The research entailed:

- Video of customers purchasing beer in stores
- Research reports of industry buying patterns
- Psychologist reports of the human brain
- Subliminal resource marketing
- Color and visual studies

I was baffled by the idea that your beer has already been pre-selected for you based on sight lines, sounds, access, laziness, and perception.

What I learned is that there is real money being spent observing our weaknesses and using our flaws to get even more money out of us. Like most people, I've heard of the astronomical cost of a thirty-second commercial during the Super Bowl. I also know the number of people watching the Super Bowl is off the charts. I now understand that as much as those ads cost, the expense is nothing compared to what they spend to get inside your head and help you believe you need that beer for a better life, not because you're thirsty.

The reality is that it is your duty to understand this is going on behind the scene in almost every item being advertised for your consumption. Once you realize what is happening, it is up to you to make the right money moves. The best way to address how you are spending your money is to ask yourself if the purchase you are preparing to make is a want or a need. Here are more questions to ask.

- Why am I buying this if it's not a need?
- Will this purchase make me money?

- Can this wait for thirty days?
- What dollars am I spending?

Money pays attention and certainly follows direction. How you place and move your money is totally up to you. Understand that what you focus on is where your mindset is and where your money is going to follow. Focus on accumulating wealth and using a percentage of the interest for your needs. This mindset will help you always be on the right side of making great money moves. Another great money move is to have multiple flows of income.

MORE MONEY FLOWS

The owner mindset isn't the only abundance mindset you can have. Generally you want to be in a controlling position when it comes to your money and time. When you consider your current financial situation to the diagram above of where people spend their time, where do you fall? If you could use more money but you are spending time or money on unproductive resources, either stop wringing your hands or refocus on more productive things after you finish your nine-to-five job.

If you need to make more money, realize you might need to

develop a new habit after work. To shore up your financial foundation, you may need to add a five-to-nine shift. Five o'clock is the time you go off the corporate clock and are on your own clock. Until now, your five-to-nine hours have been spent using up the income you have created during the nine-to-five hours. The real problem isn't that you're spending too much; it's that you don't make enough money. Let's be clear: you could be spending too much on a percentage of income basis, but my assumption is that unless you are gambling or have unhealthy habits, you just need more money.

> *"The rich invest their money and spend what is left;*
> *the poor spend their money and invest what is left."*
> Jim Rohn

Whether you are making enough to keep you where you are or you are in a financial hole, if you want to level up your life's options and choices, you need two things:

1. You must better manage what you have.
2. You must multiply your money flow.

It's critical to manage what you currently have well because when you create new money flows, it's going to go in the same direction as the past money flow. If you waste a little, you will waste a lot. You may move your finances from barely surviving in the red to thriving in the black, but if you don't manage it well, you aren't going to stay there.

One of the first things you need to do is move your mindset from a needs basis to a wants base. We've been lectured on understanding needs versus wants. But focusing only on your needs keeps you boxed in at the scarcity level. Instead, you must know what you need, focus on what you want, and be willing to work hard to get it.

I personally want financial freedom. I define financial freedom as "screw you money." That is enough money to do what I want, when I want, how I want, as often as I want. You should strive to have enough money accumulated to be able to tell your employer that if they don't value your talents and treat you fairly, you will be taking your talents to a firm that will.

The second way to level up is to multiply your money flow. Don't focus on making more money per hour or wait for that 5 percent raise to hit your checking account. Before you consider switching jobs because they are going to pay you 15 percent more and give you 50 percent more responsibility, begin to think about alternate sources of cashflow. How can you take your God-given talents and monetize them into an opportunity not only to add more money to your household but potentially replace your nine-to-five job? I don't know about you, but the chance to take more control of my destiny is right up my alley.

So what are some action steps to begin thinking outside the box?

- Take some time to research the most popular ways people are making money online.
- Make a list of what you are most interested in and whittle it down to a few opportunities.
- Research the things you whittled down to and determine how to deliver that product or service.
- Observe shortages in your life similar to other's lives and begin to formulate solutions.

What if you don't have an entrepreneurial spirit? What are some ways you can begin to brainstorm alternate forms of cashflow or jobs? The first consideration is your available time. Making more money is great as long as you, your health, and your family don't suffer. Family support in what you want to create for the family is critical. Ideas to kick around include:

- Working overtime

- Part-time work

- Teaching your expertise online

It is essential that you begin your efforts with something you like or believe that you would like. When you are working extra time, you want to be able to sustain the undertaking, so it's important to enjoy or appreciate what you will be doing.

THE RICH DON'T WORK FOR MONEY

After working in the financial service industry for so long, I have come to understand the term rich has a relative meaning. People who have never had $1,000 in their savings account think that someone with $100,000 in their savings account is rich. Someone with $100,000 thinks a million is a ton of money, and some multi-millionaires would scoff at having a mere million in the bank. Let's agree for this discussion that anyone who has over a million dollars in cash is rich. People we consider rich don't work for money. They let their money work for them.

My favorite movie quote of all time comes from the movie Wall Street. The main character tells a young protégé, "Money never sleeps, pal." To the rich, money is always changing hands and working. Their money is invested in companies and therefore always at work. In the past, the best way to grow your money was to have an invested interest in publicly traded companies like Coca-Cola. These companies literally never sleep because they are always in production and sales mode. Historically, in order to invest and make it worthwhile, you needed to have a lot of excess capital to invest. Today, you don't have to be rich to have investments around the globe; you just need an idea and a computer. You can invest as little as $25.00 per month and get into the investment world. You can also create your own means to sell items.

Late one evening years ago I was sitting in my theater room watching a movie and trying to get my PDA (personal data assistant) schedule onto my computer. I wanted it to transfer automatically, and I knew there was a way, but I didn't have the solution. After searching for hours, I excitedly came across a program that connected the two devices. I paid the $59.00, and wham, my computer and PDA were in perfect synchrony. As happy as this made me for about ten minutes, I soon became strangely irritated. I realized someone was going to wake up in the morning and have my $59.00 in their bank account. I got the program I wanted, but now I was crazy jealous. I wasn't going to wake up with a stranger's $59.00 in my account.

FINANCIALLY FREE FORMULA

The moral to the story above is that you need to have an idea or a plan that is consistently making you financially stronger. From all of my years as a financial consultant, I have created a formula that people can follow to obtain financial freedom.

My financially free formula begins with making enough money from your core job to create a surplus. Once you have a surplus, you can set aside enough money for a rainy-day emergency and then you can begin to consider additional sources of new income. Investing is the step the wealthy take to make their money work for them. Having a significant money reserve makes investing the proper way much more conducive. An investment is placing money into a resource that will increase the value of your original amount. Start with this formula and just keep repeating this process over and over.

"Master your mind, and you will always be free."

Derick Gant

The best way to secure your financial future is to recondition your mindset to think, act, and look like a millionaire. An ownership or abundance mindset will allow you to forgo frivolous purchases and put your money to work on an ongoing basis. Making sure your money has a duty, executes that duty, and attracts more money is your sole financial responsibility. What you focus on and where you spend your hard-earned money will dictate how much abundance you get to experience during your lifetime, so focus on creating more flows.

CHAPTER 8
GET IN THE BLACK

Mastering yourself includes mastering your money. The energy we expel to improve ourselves can be expressed in a variety of ways, and one measure of our efforts is the value society is willing to pay for our expertise. What we make an hour, a day, a month, or a year is what's talked about, but it's not really the measuring stick. What you should really be focused on is how much money you can keep. The first rule regarding money is that cash is king. This is the first rule because without money, you have no way to obtain your wants or needs. If you don't have money and you borrow funds from someone else, you now have more money but you don't have freedom because you owe them. Money is energy, and the more reserves you have, the more energy you create to manage, influence, and dictate your private kingdom. Simply put, money trumps and rules most of life's conditions.

I am not going to debate the age-old line, "Money can't buy you happiness." Whoever uttered that unfortunate statement must have been broke. I'll bet you anything that given the opportunity, they would never trade places with the homeless man on the corner. The same idiots who spout that phrase have misquoted the Bible when they claimed that "money is the root of all evil." In fact, the original scripture says it is the "love" of money, not money in itself, that is the root of evil. Money in and of itself is neither good nor bad.

> *"Whoever said money can't buy happiness*
> *simply didn't know where to go shopping."*
> Gertrude Stein

Let's go back to the "money can't buy you health or happiness" line. As I said, no rich person uttered that. Most people are swimming in all sorts of bills and debts, and it is the inability to pay these bills that keep them awake at night. Having the money to pay their bills would undoubtedly supply some peace of mind. Financial stress is one of the leading causes of failed marriages. The national statistics on divorce rates are alarming. What would the divorce rates be if financial burdens weren't a factor? How much happier and healthier would marriages be? Change your money, you change your world.

Money represents the gap between what we have, what we need, and what we want. The main concept of working is to close the gap of what you have and what you need. The purpose of creating multiple flows of income and thinking outside the box to accumulate more cash is to solve the shortage problem. As you bring your best while continuing to develop and improve your talents and skills, you begin to operate at a higher level, a higher value.

The problem is that even though you have raised your value by improving your talents and skills, it takes society a while to recognize and acknowledge your transformation. There is a gap between your value and your compensation. Don't worry about the gap and start delivering your best package; society will catch up and deliver your increased compensation if you stay the course. It is simply the law of supply and demand. Raise the expertise, value, and use of what you supply, and people will demand access at your price.

Just because you are waiting or working toward society recognizing your full value doesn't mean you can't make significant financial progress. Don't sit on the sidelines worried and rocking in a chair. What you need is to adopt a money code. A money code is a personal code on how you think about and handle your money. Turn what you have into a momentum-gathering force.

Making, accumulating, and retaining money can be considered a game. The purpose of the game is to fill the gaps in your life so you can fulfill your dreams. The average person doesn't have enough cash reserve to last through one or two potential pay periods. This means that almost any unexpected emergency is a real threat to their pocket. Take a minute, grab your phone, and google "how much money the average family has in savings." Next, search how much revolving debt the average family has. Once you finish your research, you will be shocked at what you learn. To remove yourself from this statistical embarrassment, you have to adopt a money code: be in the black!

What does black represent? As a color and hue, it's considered smooth and fluid, synonymous with sleek. It is also considered capable of concealing flaws and inadequacies. Black in the financial world is also symbolic. It is the word used for premium unlimited credit cards and is the term finance guys use to refer to people with an extremely high net worth. Net worth is your total assets minus your total liabilities. In layman's terms, it is how much cash and value you have after all the bills and debts are paid. The phrase "in the black" is widely used to refer to the condition of companies that have been profitable in their latest accounting period.

"In the black" in terms of a 24K Life Code represents an absolute abundance of balance in your spiritual, mental, physical, and financial life. Consider striving to have more than a lot of money; aim to have an abundant life by delivering your best self over and over. In this chapter we will focus how to get your finances in the black quickly.

STOP THE BLEEDING

There are many times I get calls from hardworking families that are drowning financially. They are behind on the household bills or credit cards, and they are in fear of losing their home or car. Let's be realistic: the average household doesn't have $500 in any account to fall back on, so things can get dire fast. In these cases, there is little time, attention, or desire to pull out the old budget sheet and reorganize their finances. Some situations are critical and call for immediate action. In an emergency, the biggest issue is to stop the bleeding and assess the damage.

If you are serious about making an aggressive change, the best way to proceed is to cease and desist all nonessential spending. Freeze all subscriptions, kids' phones and devices, the cable, and memberships. Minimize your Wi-Fi and phone plans. Eliminate all outside dining and entertainment.

Once this is done, make a list of the bills that are due, and map out the funds that can be used to attack the expenses for the next three pay periods. With your financial information in hand, you should be able to contact your creditors and make payment arrangements. Pay core bill first, allocate funds for personal care second, and address anything you can thereafter.

The most important step to stopping the bleeding is to use a concept called cash and carry. When you need to make a purchase, the only way you can do it is by paying for the item in full with cash. If you don't have cash, you can't buy the item. This strategy works best for impulse buyers.

Any core purchase should come as the result of being placed on a list. Any purchase over a few hundred dollars should be planned out. Cash and carry includes no cash advances, credit card purchases, or borrowed funds. To truly get a handle on the bleeding, drastic measures must be taken.

> *"Rich people have small TVs and big libraries,*
> *and poor people have small libraries and big TVs."*
> Zig Ziglar

MONEY DOESN'T GROW ON TREES

Perhaps some of our parents didn't know much about money management, but they could have shared some basic financial lessons that could've spared us a lot of costly lessons. Unfortunately, money and the discussion of money is taboo in many homes and within society at large. In the home, no one dares ask their parents how much they make.

I recall my dad saying millions of times, "Money doesn't grow on trees." The universal monetary translation of that quote is, "No, you can't have any money because money is scarce." I'm sure you have heard the same phrase or some variation of it as a kid. Though my dad was a great provider, there were times the city water department came out and shut off the water to the house due to nonpayment. He would come home from a long day, tired and gruff, only to find out there was no water. Being a master plumber, he had a device that simply switched it back on, but we never dared ask why the bill didn't get paid.

Understanding that money matters begins in the home, and it is vital that we remove the stigma that talking about money is wrong. Money is at the center of almost everything that happens. When looking to set your money code, consider your personal finances like you are doing a strategic deal. Every individual transaction you make has a positive or negative value. This includes fitness, church, groceries, and furniture. Companies continuously and strategically analyze their financial positions daily, and you should do the same with your personal financial position.

Be Personally Profitable

Companies operate to create and maintain a profit. They cut liabilities, invest in appreciating assets, and hire employees who increase the company value. Capital expenditures are limited to items needed to pump up the bottom line only when capacity has been met and exceeded. Translate this into your personal life. Every purchase you make should be made on a needs basis and should keep your household moving efficiently. Purchases made from a wants basis drain profits and reduce the potential for saving and investing more money.

Many families have extended family or friends who ask for or cost them money. These are the folks who spend every dime they make and charge what they don't have. They have borrowed from you twenty times with the promise to repay you but somehow never have the money to do so. I understand that these are people in our lives whom we love, but they are draining your success. Because it is nearly impossible for you to tell them no, set up a special benevolence account and designate a specific amount that you are willing to help others with. Once the benevolent account is empty for the year, that is the end of your giving. Success is a choice on your part as much as it is theirs.

Think about reducing the things that have no profitable result but totally function as an ego-based luxury. In my budget it might be upgrading to the latest iPhone or 5G television. Focus on how much money you could save eliminating wasteful spending and re-direct it to an appreciating asset. Every expense has an opportunity to appreciate or depreciate your personal net worth. What you focus on grows exponentially, so stay focused on positive expansion. This means you spend money on things that appreciate or help you make more money. Remember that your money code is a system capable of handling a few thousand or a few million dollars.

I am not adopting or promoting a scarcity mindset; precisely the opposite. Think expansion and abundance. You might be fooled into thinking that tracking your money is living in fear of spending or wasting. It isn't. Tracking your income and expenses is a way for you to make educated and informed decisions about the best way to grow your financial life. The goal is to understand where your money is going and assign a responsibility to each dollar. Get more of your dollars working in house versus going out of the house.

Don't worry about when your big payday is coming. Every successful corporation graciously compensates their top producers and often includes massive bonuses. Your bonus check is coming as the owner of your business. The key is to know what funds are available for bonuses and what funds are needed to grow your life.

Track Your Numbers

Measure your resources by creating a personal budget, a balance sheet, and a net worth statement. You want to look great on paper and even better in real life. The question you need to answer is this: If you had the chance, would you invest in your company (household)? An excellent investment is a household that is making a lot of revenue, has minimum bad debt, and has piles of retained earnings or cash on hand, and that's what you want for your personal finances as well.

The smart money move is to reorganize your finances and get it in the black. Your personal income needs to cover all of your monthly expenses with funds remaining to fund several accounts:

1. Three months' expenses (emergency)

2. Vacations

3. Home improvements

4. Short-term needs

5. Long-term needs (college funds and retirement, for example)

It's important to be informed and educated in making any big decision. It's okay to make a decision contrary to conventional wisdom, but it's not okay to make a decision blind or out of ignorance. Reorganizing your finances and consistently tracking your numbers will be monotonous at first. This process may even seem depressing if you are struggling financially. Fight through the urge to put it aside and work on it later; what you focus on will get your best ideas and attention. Things will turn around much sooner than you think they will.

GET ACCREDITED

The measurement the government uses to determine personal financial stability that you may have never heard of is an accredited investor. In the United States, to be considered an accredited investor, one must have a net worth of at least $1,000,000, excluding the value of one's primary residence, or have income of at least $200,000 each year for the last two years (or $300,000 combined income, if married) and have the expectation to make the same amount moving forward.

$100,000 + 800 Credit Score
$10,000 + 700 Credit Score
Even - $1,000

As an accredited investor, you have insulated your life and finances enough that you can afford to take risks in more advanced-type investments. There are investments that are considered more sophisticated and potentially risky. Mostly these deals are private and offer a higher potential return over pedestrian investment opportunities. There are levels to building your financial life. The accredited investor level is in the middle of the wealth-building chart.

Having a consistent money code will lead you to becoming an accredited investor. The key is to educate yourself or find a professional who can help you along the way to achieve this level. If you suddenly came into a million dollars, you would likely lose it if you didn't prepare yourself to handle it properly. Being an accredited investor is definitely living your life in the black.

"Money is only a tool. It will take you wherever you wish, but it will not replace you as the driver."

Ayn Rand

It is imperative to understand that you want and need to be in the black to obtain financial freedom. Just keep playing the game, keep improving, be your best, and the money will catch up. Raise you talent and skills so high that you become an expert and everyone in town wants you to grace them with your service. The 24K Life, baby!

CHAPTER 9
PAY YOURSELF FIRST

Your bonus is coming, but waiting to experience the rewards of your hard work can be defeating in and of itself. Along this tough climb to improving and leveling up your life, you have to see consistent wins along the way. If you plow through without appreciating the wins, you may burn out and quit. We have all heard the old adage of paying yourself first, but it's rarely explained and definitely not taught in practical terms.

GRANDAD'S THREE CANS

My maternal grandfather was a significant influence on my life when it comes to business and money. He would always say you don't spend money you don't have. He taught by example, always having cash on hand in a pinch. He didn't tell me how to pay myself first, but I learned by watching him as he operated his barbershop. When it came to working, my grandfather didn't play games or favorites. I remember my father trying to get a free haircut every now and again for himself or my brother and me. That never happened.

One of my first jobs was sweeping up all of the hair on the floor in his shop. I watched my grandfather manage clients and his money. After several clients paid, he would go in the back behind a curtain and place a portion of the proceeds in a Hills Bros. coffee can, a part in a Maxwell House can, and the remaining portion in a Folgers can. The money from one can was deposited into the bank, the money in another went home, and no one knew where the money in the final can went. Later we learned it was his profit-first can, his pay yourself first can. We found the cans in storage boxes on his passing; he had thousands and thousands tucked away.

JOHN'S THREE CIRCLES

When I was hired and joined Savage and Associates financial planning firm as a consultant, the first thing I was taught was John Savage's three circles of financial success.

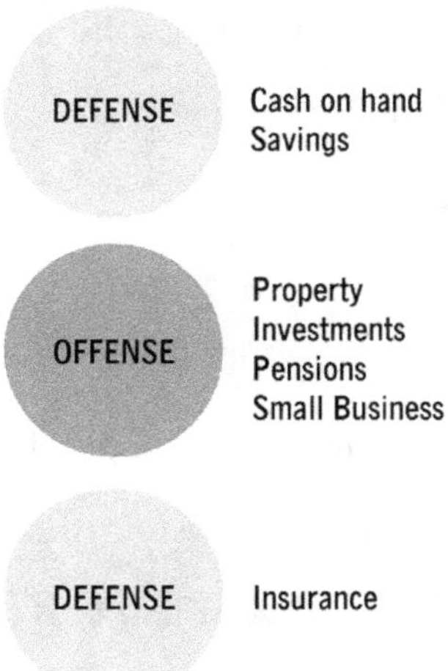

The first circle represents a personal bank account where paychecks are deposited and allocated in this order:

1. Savings for yourself

2. Household bills

3. Family, food, fun

4. Vacations

The second circle is specifically for all appreciating assets:

1. Home purchase

2. Pension and retirement

3. Starting a business

4. Stocks/bonds/investing

The third circle is for establishing a solid insurances defense like:

1. Life/health/disability

2. Home and auto

3. Long-term care

The three-circle financial philosophy is to create a solid defense with the first and third circles. Cash in the bank representing your personal reserve for you and your family is a protection against unforeseen life circumstances. The bank account in actuality is a series of accounts that represent a bill payment account, a personal savings account, and your personal needs account. The process is boring because progress happens slowly over each and every pay period. Each pay period or each month, you deposit a portion of your income into each account and watch it grow.

The second circle is where you deposit any and all discretionary funds to invest in any asset that grows in value. Traditionally the largest asset anyone has is their personal residence. The second largest asset for most is their 401(k) pension plan. These two assets are the largest mostly in part because there is no easy way to get funds out of the assets. You can't easily ask your house to give you $200.00 for a nice night out on the town. Left undisturbed, these assets are consistently accumulating wealth with every deposit.

The three circles have been successfully taught to thousands of advisors and millions of families. The base money code is to pay yourself first and invest in appreciating assets while minimizing waste. A great idea.

PERFECTING YOUR CANS

In order to have a sound financial life, you are going to have to determine the maximum amount of funds available for yourself, investing, and play. Knowing how much discretionary income you have is necessary to learning how much you can pay yourself first.

Discretionary income is the remaining funds after you've itemized your income and expenses. We all wish we could pay ourselves our entire check, but that isn't realistic. You have accumulated expenses, and you only have a certain amount of income. Once you know what is remaining, this number can be systematically taken off the top once your paycheck hits your account. You can separate your direct-deposit funds into the separate accounts described below. Having your funds automatically separated into accounts is preferred. Just like your house and your pension contributions, out of sight, out of mind means more money free to accumulate.

The Do not Touch savings account needs to be a one-way account. This means the money goes in, but it's challenging to get out. Most people have no savings because it's the first account they attack when they have a slight spending urge. To avoid raiding your savings, I suggest you have multiple savings accounts:

1. A Do Not Touch account (emergency fund)

2. A Short-Term Spending fund (birthday/Christmas/quarterly payments)

3. A Capital Purchase account (home repair, a car, new TV, etc.)

4. Next Level fund (after-tax investments)

The psychology behind the multiple accounts is that you will have to make a conscious decision on which area you are going to have to pull money from when you have an unplanned expense. There is no question that when it's time to pull funds for a planned expense, the money is in the appropriate account. The tough part is when you need or want something that wasn't foreseen or planned.

Taking the emergency fund off the table as a choice for any wants is a critical step. Having those funds protected is vital to your-long term financial health.

The best place to pay yourself first is to contribute to a pre-tax retirement account. It's the wisest because the money never hits your hands, the tax is postponed into the future, and usually the rules to take the funds out are difficult enough to dissuade frivolous withdrawals. There are other ways to pay yourself first financially, but the universal secret to amassing any real pot of gold is to systematically divert those funds and never touch the pot.

Paying yourself first is a long-term play. It is not a "reward yourself first" concept. Spending wastefully on meaningless items soothes a very temporary high, but it is also the fastest route to maintaining a middle-income lifestyle.

> *"Following the pay yourself first rule is more a matter*
> *of self-discipline than anything else."*
> Robert Kiyosaki

SAY YES TO YOURSELF

There is a big difference between being asked for money and being asked to waste money. I mentioned setting up the benevolence account for those you love and truly want to help. The test comes when your family and friends who never plan or budget regularly ask you to go out to dinner or go out for drinks. The perception of being able to hang out on a whim is an important social construct for most people. Before now, you had no clue how much you really spent on these excursions, but now you do. For years you have said yes, but now that you genuinely want to live a 24K Life, you have to say no. To be honest, I'd prefer you look at this scenario as saying yes to yourself, not saying no to someone else.

I consider Team Gant first in every difficult money challenge or decision. When a situation arises, I ask myself if it is good for the team. If the answer is no, then I say yes to the team, and let anything and everyone else go out on their own.

Of course, this breeds negative feelings and actions from others. They want you to waste your money as they do. No one wants to be a loser alone, hence the saying, "Misery loves company." You have to have the moxie and the courage to stand alone on top of your values, principles, and master plans. Without a strategy, purpose, and plan, it is nearly impossible to follow your money mindset consistently. People are against you, advertisers are against you, and the system is against you. They all want access to every dime you earn or can borrow. This is why it's essential to live by your money code.

POSITION YOURSELF PROPERLY

Self-improvement takes a ton of work and tremendous drive. Things like putting yourself first or telling friends no may sound easy, but if it were, you would have done this a long time ago. The human will to prevail and to overcome adversity is in all of us. The question is, what is the trigger that finally lights the fuse to set your soul on fire to take a leap into greatness?

So many people are stuck in their story of failure and abuse that they fail to see the story of their future greatness and glory. Both exist; it's just a matter of which you choose to focus on. I am not who you met yesterday. I am a wiser, stronger, smarter, and a hungrier version of my best self. What are you hungry for, or are you just starving on the past?

When I worked for a prominent consulting firm, it was understood that the firm always came first. It was assumed and expected that everyone lived by the philosophy that the sum was greater than the parts. The next in line to benefit was the client, and of course, the consultant was last. I hated this because no one was looking out for my best interest and had no real concern of my financial welfare. I adopted my own unspoken hierarchy, and it placed the client first, myself second, and the firm third.

After years of putting myself third in the business world, I applied the principle to pay myself first. When you work for someone else, it can be challenging to find ways to put yourself first and keep your job. The best way to accomplish this is to outperform everyone to the extreme. When you outperform your coworkers and peers, everything you do for the company is golden. You have made yourself a producer or the golden goose. This directly ties into putting yourself first because when you are at the top, you get to set precedents and change rules. Putting yourself first places you in the position where others are striving to help you be even better and accommodate you to do even more. Once you have successfully accomplished this, believe me, they will leave you alone. Success follows success, and as long as it's legal, everyone is all in!

Unfortunately, I didn't become the top producer, but what I did do was change the way the game was viewed. The firm had no fee-based consultants. Everyone was a commission-only representative. As a commission-based advisor, the company got their immediate commission override, the client got their investment, and I got my cut of the commission. All of them were short-term game plans. I jumped in the fee-based world where I could get a consistent stream of income, serve the client, and let the firm get their override. Becoming a fee-based advisor was great for my pay yourself first strategy because the clients were happy to have reduced fees and I was at peace not feeling like I was selling for a commission on every conversation. Paying yourself first is at times about doing the things that make you the most happy first.

Placing yourself first, the client second, and everyone else third is fine if your intent is pure. Always have something of substance and value to offer clients and they will be first in their eyes. Putting yourself first doesn't mean you are a greedy bastard. It doesn't mean you don't care about anyone else. You have to be a good egg no matter what order you come in the line-up. If you are a rotten egg, you're going to be bad at whichever order you choose.

The Best Way to Help Others

If you don't first succeed, you can't help anyone.

"The best way to help the poor is not to be one of them."
John F. Savage

If you are broke, busted, and defeated, how are you going to bring your best to any situation that needs all you have to offer? It is your duty, your obligation, to be as stable and steadfast as possible. Placing yourself first is building your base on a rock in order to survive and thrive through any storm or tough times. This is a hard concept for so many people to act on. Just as when you're in a plane and the attendant instructs you to place your oxygen mask on first, you have to take care of yourself first.

When you place yourself anywhere other than first, you run the risk of diminishing your personal value or self-worth. Telling yourself that you can accept what's left or what's not in your best interest slowly begins to prevail and become your life.

For many years I was so concerned with helping people overcome financial despair that I would literally give services and time away. Wanting to see them win, to see them get out from under the pain and suffering economic weights, was very important to me. Many times the results were that clients would take advantage of my generosity and ask for more freebies as well as more time. Because I had set a precedent, they felt justified and even got upset whenever I refused to give away any more services for free.

It would be misleading if I didn't address the fact that this is one of the most challenging transformations to make. Somewhere in our money mindset and self-worth value system, we were unduly convinced that we are not worth much. Maybe this wasn't done intentionally, but the ramifications are devastating to your life and future.

Historically, if you were not wealthy, you were not allowed some of the basic freedoms of life. Women usually didn't work outside the home until World War II, minorities couldn't vote or own land, and everyone in the bottom 90 percent of income earners was paid just enough to borrow funds to beg for a home loan. Modern economics are tied like an albatross to the neck of the middle class. The middle class lives under a curse of average income and massive consumption while grinding for the American Dream is encouraged.

> *"Without wisdom, gold is quickly lost by those who have it."*
> George S. Clason

Modern economics, however, is a choice. No one is forced to spend their first dollar and save what's remaining. There is very little formal personal financial literacy taught in schools. However, as of April 2019, 56.1 percent of the world's population has internet access, and 81 percent of the developed world has internet access.[16] With that kind of access, there are few excuses for anyone not knowing how to financially or otherwise improve their life.

PART III
REFINING GOLD

CHAPTER 10
OVERCOMING ADVERSITY

Each of us has to mentally prepare to win as much as we must be prepared to fail. Times will not always flow in our favor, so having your armor or defenses ready is a wise move. There are four key factors I consider to keep me sane when facing a negative flow, poor trend, or just life's problems. First of all, money solves most problems, so I focus on where I am financially and how my current situation is related to money. The second thing I consider is if the problem is within my control. Inevitably, whether it is in my control or not, I revert to controlling everything in my life that I believe I can and this helps me gain a stronger sense of success.

The next option I understand but never consider is giving up. From the time I was a toddler, I was never allowed to give up, and it is just super hard for me to even entertain the idea now. Finally, of all the wise moves I could make, recalibrating my plan is number one. When things are moving against us, a close look at what's wrong, especially in the details, is key. Once you can identify what's off, you can begin to make the necessary corrections.

"Only those who dare to fail greatly can ever achieve greatly."
Robert Kennedy

MONEY SOLVES MOST PROBLEMS

When you are feeling a pinch, it's time to make more money. When you realize that money is energy and provides access to education, connections, resources, and opportunities, you will have learned a precious life lesson.

Spending money is the start to most of life's transactions. Think about it. No matter what you do, you need access to a money. Let's say you want to stop and smell the roses one sunny afternoon. If you take a walk in the park or the botanical garden, free no charge, you may think, Everything doesn't cost money.

Wrong.

What does it take to provide you access to those flowers? How did you get to the flowers? Did you take a taxi? Drive your car? If you walked, did you wear clothes and shoes? Money makes the world, more specifically, your world, go around.

Managing your money better will also help you function better in society. Managing your money means you won't have to continuously stress over not having any and worrying where your next demand of life is going to come from.

"While money can't buy happiness, it certainly lets you choose your own form of misery."
Groucho Marx

Creating and managing your money keeps you in a favorable cash position and in power. Managing your money means that your life is somewhat organized as well. People who manage their money know what and when funds are available for the next need or want. This keeps them in control of what's next with less stress.

When you think about the major issues in your life, what are they? When I was in my late twenty's, mine looked something like:

- How will my family fair if I die prematurely?

- How can I best send my boys to college?

- My car is on its last leg. How much can I afford for a new one?

- My chest feels funny, but my medical co-pay deductible is $1,000.

- I need to get into shape.

- I have to join a gym and get some clothes.

Pick your top concerns and determine what the best solution is for you and your family. The majority of the answers are going to be more money. I don't consider this a bad thing; it's just the reality of our society. Most things cost money. I didn't list any frivolous concerns about vacation or entertainment. My questions addressed real-life issues because we were already aware that the other stuff came with a price tag too.

Is This Something I Can Control?

When faced with a dilemma, the question to ask yourself is simply, "Is this situation something within my control?" Unless you are superhuman or a meta-human, we all have specific limitations.

One way to keep yourself in the game is to ask yourself this question at every opportunity. No matter the situation, when you ask this question, you are forced to take inventory and ownership of your responsibilities and actions.

If you answer this question yes, you have choices to make as well as more questions to answer:

1. What is my next best move to handle this?

2. What are all of my options?

3. Can I get help with this?

There are a host of questions to ask yourself to drill down to what can be done today to begin to solve that issue. I hope it is evident that you cannot control anyone else, so you should never answer, "Yes, if so and so cooperates." You can only control yourself and the actions you decide to take.

It is vital that you take radical ownership for where you are at the very moment. If you are one of those people who have a great excuse for everything and it involves some outside force to blame for why you missed your mark, good luck, but this book most likely won't help you. Each of us is where we are by the decisions we have made throughout our lives. Own your shit, and your life will take a completely different path moving forward.

I remember when I divorced, one of my first thoughts was, Now I can work until midnight or go to the gym without any complaints holding me back. That sounded great until the reality hit that I worked the same hours and attended the gym the same amount of times. No one but me had been holding me back.

"Destiny is no matter of chance. It is a matter of choice. It is not a thing to be waited for, it is a thing to be achieved."

William Jennings Bryan

Your success and potential are in your hands. Own it 100 percent and operate in your power from sunup to sundown. Answering yes to the question, "Is this within my control?" is not comfortable or pleasant. Radical ownership and self-responsibility are big jobs that most people pass on. But when you forgo handling your business and your responsibilities, problems begin to grow and become insurmountable.

What if the answer to the question "Is this within your control?" is no? Logic would have it that if I can't control a situation, then I should just let it be and move on. But how easy is it to admit a lack of control and how difficult is it to just let go of a situation? If it were easy, no one would worry or stress out. There is an art to understanding how to operate when you realize a situation is out of your control. When faced with this reality, I consider the magnitude and power of life and what my place is in the puzzle. I often rely on the imagery I create from this thought: I can't do God's work, and he won't do mine!

I can't create miracles or hypnotize others to do my bidding. What I imagine when I say this to myself is that it is 100 percent my responsibility to do what I can do to the best with my ability. God is not going to go to the gym for me or cook healthy meals for me. He is not going to take a portion of my pay and place it in a savings account so future me will have plenty of money.

Understanding that you can't control a situation is the first step, and practicing letting go is the second. It takes time and consistent consideration to let things be and to only own your part. There is no easy way to explain how I graduated to letting the things go I can't control. The process I incorporated was to thoroughly think about the original question. Once I realize I can't do anything about a situation, my belief that God or a higher power has a plan and the ability to see me through the situation to a successful conclusion allows me to let go.

In these times, I pray and position myself to be strong enough to withstand the pain or relief of the result. If you can't seem to do this, I suggest you recall past situations that seemed unbearable and tragic. Remember what happened and how you survived the duration. There are times that the most unbearable circumstances have crippled people physically or mentally. If you are standing and sane, you made it and are making it. Keep believing and standing in your strength.

Never Say Uncle

It's cute and supportive when people post memes that say, "Never Quit," but how exactly do you preserve when you are exhausted or at a loss as to what your next move should be? Our biggest day-to-day challenge is to preserve. As long as you have your health and others know and reward your value, life is good, and it's somewhat easy to keep pressing on. In the investment world, we have a saying: "The trend is your friend." This simply means when you can spot a regular flow, you can adjust and ride that trend or wave until it changes. This applies to all areas of life as well as business. The phrase "Don't rock the boat" is a perfect example, meaning when things are good and working in your favor, don't do anything to mess it up. You can easily go with the flow when life is great, but what happens when the trend changes and the flow is not really flowing or it's flowing against you?

One effective way to never quit is to focus your attention on regular small wins. Setting small goals that lead to your larger goals is strategically smart. Achieving small victories lets you know that you are on the right path and that you are positioned for success. Winning has powerful psychological effects that boost one's self-esteem. Consistently winning changes your story and redefines you as a winner, someone who accomplishes things and exceeds expectations.

"It always seems impossible until it's done."
Nelson Mandela

Changing your inner game has a direct effect on the success of your outer results. Never saying uncle is more about the ongoing conversation you have inside of your head. The more you think and talk to yourself about quitting, the more your brain configures reasons and ways for that to happen.

We talked about this earlier, but we are all built on the story we tell ourselves. The key is to tell yourself a story that is optimistic and hopeful. Tell a story that remembers the good, the wins, the triumphs. We all tend to recall the tough times, the losses, the times we came up short. Luckily with the knowledge of how the brain works and consistent effort toward small wins, we can change the desire to quit to one of pressing forward.

Recalibrate the Engine

When you are driving and striving for greatness, you need to assess and reassess your efforts and results. The key is to consistently calibrate and recalibrate where you are and where you are going. We like to think that just because we tried to win, our energy is honorable. Not so. The only thing that matters in the real world are results. No one cares how steep the road was if you lose.

The key to overcoming adversity is to successfully implement a recalibration system. Recalibrating is fine-tuning how to:

- Make more money
- Ask yourself if this is something you can control
- Remind yourself to never quit

When you recalibrate, you are checking how well your decisions are working for you. If you find they are working great, keep pressing along, occasionally asking yourself how you can make your situation even better. When things aren't working so great, it's best to dissect the circumstances and figure out how to make them work better as fast as possible.

Set daily goals and review them at the end of the day to make sure that if you fell short, you can adjust and reset for the next day. If you conquered and met the mark that day, you can reset and create more significant goals to reach for tomorrow.

You are the engine that makes your world go. Do all you can to stay out of the darkness; it's too tough to get back into the light.

CHAPTER 11
CREATING PEAK PERFORMANCE

When you look to live your best life, you have to be prepared to expend a lot of energy. With this in mind, it is imperative to understand the principles to get your physical body into prime shape so you can deliver your peak performance. Based on the information I have learned, I created lifestyle habits to efficiently maintain my body in a peak performance state. I have knowledge and opinions about the body, but by no means am I an expert on anyone's body except my own. I am providing the information I know to be essential to the average person's health and maintenance. Mind, body, and spirit must all be consistently cared for to have a balanced life, a 24K Life. When you are out of alignment in one of these areas, life seems to be a bit off-center. Your journey is to master yourself and know what works best for your personal success.

"You cannot dream yourself into a character;
you must hammer and forge yourself one."
James Froude

I have exercised five out of seven days most of my life, so it has become a foundational part of who I am. There have, however, been long periods when I fell completely off the wagon and ended up twenty to thirty pounds overweight. Thankfully those days are few and far between from my typical modus operandi. One of the reasons I can remain in peak shape is because I know my weaknesses, and I operate around them as best I can. I don't keep certain foods in the house, I don't eat a full meal past a particular hour, and I don't go three days in a row without exercise. The result is that I stay well within a range of weight and fitness that I require to attack life daily.

Over the years I have tracked what meal plans, exercises, and activities have worked best for me. With time comes change, and as

I age what used to work like a charm doesn't have the same results any longer. This means I have to continuously alter and adjust what is working and most importantly, what's not working. Much like anything worth doing, we have to continually change in order to make improvements.

Consider every physical area of your life that must be attended to in order to operate at a peak level. It's amazing how much mental work drains the physical body. It has been proven there is a definite mind–body connection and that mental fatigue can cause physical fatigue as well. It didn't take a science report for me to realize my daily conditioning impacts my performance in all areas of my life.

Transformation takes consistent effort. Living your best life, a 24K Life, takes a tremendous amount of courage and focus. Performing at a level that is greater than the norm takes mental and physical energy.

Peak performance includes your physical training, nutrition, health checks, and most importantly, your sleeping habits. These things must be evaluated and adjusted to maintain a 24K Life balance.

PHYSICAL TRAINING

By the time you are thirty-five, you have had many life experiences, you make smarter decisions, and you are probably a bit more easygoing than you were in your twenties. While your decisions and choices improve with age, unfortunately your muscle mass can falter. About the age of thirty-five you start to lose muscle mass if you don't regularly work out. Less muscle means daily activities like lifting furniture, doing yard work, or playing with your kids can become a problem.

We are all aware that the older you get, the more unstable you can be and the more likely injury is possible if you fall. You must use muscle or you will lose it. If you are sitting around and not exercising and moving, you are going to lose muscle. Commit to working out a few times a week; it can make a huge difference.

You may be wondering what the best type of exercise is to lose weight. There isn't one kind of workout that's better than the others. A balanced workout routine should include a combination of three types of exercise for weight loss: aerobic exercise, strength training, and flexibility exercises.

AEROBIC EXERCISE

Aerobic exercise can be called cardiovascular training or cardio. Cardio exercise significantly raises your heart rate. Spinning, swimming, running, and walking are all cardiovascular activities. When you cardio train, you go into hyperdrive and speed up your inner engine. When you exercise enough, you burn fat and calories both during and after exercise.

I recommend getting a quality physical checkup and then get a quality heart rate monitor and make a game of tracking your progress. Don't forget to change your story. If you have never been an exercise person or you have taken an extended hiatus, don't begin by telling yourself how hard it's going to be. Begin to confirm in your mind that you can do this and you will be so much better for it.

Start slow and progress to more aggressive sessions. In David Goggins's book Can't Hurt Me[17] he talks about how he started running from the house to the first telephone pole on his street and then back to the house. The next time he ran to the second pole out and then the third, and kept increasing his distance until he had transformed himself into the baddest man on the planet. David was an out-of-shape guy with no motivation until he decided that he was no longer going to be that guy and took some action. You are equally able to change your story, your mind, and your life!

Strength Training

Strength training builds muscle. Strength training is also known as lifting weights. Sometimes people who are trying to lose weight will skip weight lifting because they want to lose weight and don't think lifting weights will help them drop pounds. Lifting weights is a big factor in losing inches and eventually pounds. Muscle is denser than fat; however, muscle helps the body burn fat. A body with more muscle tends to burns more calories even when it's at rest. This makes it ideal to include in your training routine.

Many women find that in their forties weight gain is almost inevitable and weight loss is impossible. But women who continue to build and maintain muscle are less likely to suffer from this problem. I have found when I teach spin class that many women are afraid of losing their feminine look, so they avoid lifting weights. But the older we get, the more we need the strength to do life's basics.

The amount of weight lifting required to change one's physique to muscular is much higher than people think. If you're scared but want to do some strength exercises to lose weight, start by doing a simple weight-training program at home. Start by targeting your arms, legs, and abs with an easy online routine that takes just twenty to thirty minutes, two to three times a week.

FLEXIBILITY EXERCISES

Flexibility training or stretching becomes more critical as age creeps up. Stretching is often neglected as part of a workout routine. Stretching helps us maintain a good range of motion, remain loose, and keep our balance. But the most significant benefit of stretching is that it relieves stress. An effective stretching program takes a small amount of time and can be done just about anywhere. When you get a massage or a good stretch, it makes everything feel so much better.

Take the time to establish a simple morning routine shortly after waking and getting up. A ten-minute stretch every morning will allow your blood to circulate, getting oxygen to all of your body parts and establishing a baseline for a balanced day.

COMBINE ALL THREE

A 24K Life physical training routine should include all three primary forms. You now know why each kind of training matters, so be sure you add some focus on all three areas into your complete weekly plan. Working out doesn't require a considerable time investment. If you currently participate in some cardio programs, add some strength training on a few of those days and stretching at the end of each session. Making this adjustment and investment will help you enjoy big rewards when it's time to step on the scale or shovel a little snow.

ABS OF STEEL

Most people want a solid midsection. But why is it so hard to trim down and tone up your mid-section? What's the real deal about your core? I'm going to give you a better picture of your core.

First, let me ask you a question. Are you doing any regular exercise for an extended period? What you focus on expands, so if you are not taking the time to do the work, don't expect any real results. You may be doing sit-ups, crunches, and side bends, hoping to flatten your stomach, but if you haven't been consistent, you just keep starting over from the beginning. When you do core exercises like sit-ups, your muscles get sore, which makes you think you're strengthening your abs.

People assume your core is made to crunch, twist, and bend, but in reality, it's the complete opposite. The purpose of your abdominal muscles is to prevent your midsection from crunching, twisting, and turning. Your core is a stabilizer designed to protect your spine. So even though you feel the burn, you are doing more harm than good.

If you want to get a better, tighter midsection, do a complete core exercise like:

- Planks
- Seated bicycles
- Seated Leg Lifts
- V – Ups

Your stomach is only one part of your core, and to go from flabby to fit, you must strengthen your core and all of the muscles surrounding it.

The next important component to shrinking your abs is to put down the sugar. Sugar is the number one reason people carry fat on their stomach. This is because sugar stimulates a fat-storing hormone called insulin. So the more sugar you eat, the more insulin your body secretes, and that means you gain more fat. All carbohydrates break down into sugar once they're in your body. That's why foods like bread, pasta, and rice make you pack on the pounds and cause you to feel bloated at times.

Have you ever felt like you always are working out but can't lose any weight? If you want to lean down, you also must wake up your metabolism! Your metabolism works around the clock to keep your body functioning optimally, and it requires fuel to keep running. The fuel that keeps the body going is fat. So by increasing your metabolism, you're telling your body to burn off fat. One way to get your metabolism going is to add in some interval training. HIIT (high-intensity interval training) is also called metabolic training, and it involves exercises that working more of your muscle, which creates a more significant energy boost, demanding more fat to be burned for fuel. HIIT training is any exercise where you push your heart rate hard for short periods of time with less-intense recovery periods. This can be in a group exercise class or done alone running on a treadmill.

NUTRITION

You can't out-exercise a bad diet. A proper diet is needed to get the right amount of each nutrient in your body. There are five primary nutrients the body needs to survive:

- Carbohydrates

- Fats

- Proteins

- Vitamins and minerals

CARBOHYDRATES

Carbohydrates create energy in our bodies. They break down to glucose in your stomach and are used as fuel. Carbohydrates are found in the sweet and starchy foods we love, items such as bananas, breads, rice, potatoes, and spaghetti. There are carbohydrates that are more efficient fuels such as:

- Vegetables: All of them

- Whole fruits: Apples, bananas, strawberries, etc.

- Legumes: Lentils, kidney beans, peas, etc.

- Nuts: Almonds, walnuts, hazelnuts, macadamia nuts, peanuts, etc.

- Seeds: Chia seeds, pumpkin seeds.

- Whole grains: Choose grains that are truly whole, as in pure oats, quinoa, brown rice, etc.

FATS

Fats are also used for energy. We get our muscle growth from a mixture of fats and glycogen. Fat is found in butter, olive oil and other cooking oils, meat, nuts, and cream.

PROTEINS

Our bodies need protein to build cells, to make blood, and to restore and repair tissues. Protein is found in meat, eggs, fish, beans, peas, lentils, and nuts. Our bodies can also use protein for energy, but only if it has run out of carbohydrates and fats.

FIBER

Fiber is a substance called cellulose from the cell walls of plants. You find it in fruits, veggies, brown bread, bran, and other cereals. You cannot digest it. It passes straight through the stomach and is excreted as feces. Even though fiber can't be digested, it is essential because it helps the body digestive system function properly.

VITAMINS AND MINERALS

Our bodies need small amounts of vitamins. Some can be stored in your liver; others, like vitamin C, can't be stored. When you eat more than you need, the extra is excreted. Minerals are just as essential as vitamins. There is enough iron in our bodies to make a nail.[18] Without iron your blood can't carry oxygen and without calcium you'd have no bones, teeth, or muscle contractions. Minerals are an essential part of an efficient body. They are involved in almost all enzyme reactions in the body. Without enzyme activity, life does not exist.

Your good health lies in the proper mineral intake and ideal mineral ratios. Anything else you do for your health is excellent, but minerals must be the priority. Having a balanced and stable mineral level solves the majority of health issues people attempt to correct by other means. Many minerals need to be replenished, while other minerals need to be detoxed if they are forms the body cannot utilize.

UNLOCKING YOUR PEAK PERFORMANCE

I asked a good friend of mine and former professional athlete Jimmy Jackson the most efficient way he learned how to get the most out of his body. I expected him to tell me about all of the sophisticated strategies and techniques he had learned from his experiences as an NBA player. I wanted the inside scoop from the best trainers in the world who fine-tuned the best athletes in the world. What he told me was incredibly simple.

Bubby Corggens, a local fitness guru who worked with Jimmy, had him take a hair tissue mineral analysis. A hair tissue mineral analysis (HTMA), which only cost $100, told him the entire story of his optimal nutritional performance. Bubby explained that we are all different and have different dietary needs and deficiencies. Your physical and cognitive abilities can be analyzed using hair tissue mineral analysis.

Nutrient mineral levels and their ratios determine how well your cells function and impact physical and cognitive performance. The goal of HTMA is to correct body chemistry and improve cell functioning, using it as a guide for targeted supplementation.

HTMA is focused on a nutrient-rich diet, targeted supplement therapy, detoxification, and learning to avoid things that cause you harm. The benefits include improved cognitive function, more energy, correcting the metabolic rate (weight loss), emotional stability, and higher stress resilience.

A hair mineral analysis provides a picture of body chemistry, including:
- Heavy metal toxicity

- Mineral deficiencies and imbalances

- Metabolic rate (fast or slow)

- Adrenal fatigue

- Thyroid function

- Nervous system imbalances

- Protein synthesis

- Inflammation

- Energy levels

- Mental health issues

- Liver and kidney stress

- Carbohydrate tolerance

- Blood sugar imbalances

- Insulin resistance

The reality is that knowledge is power and with this information you can unlock the key to your personal body chemistry. The information gained by going through this analysis is one more step to identifying your uniqueness and determining what will help you perform at a higher level.

WATER

Water doesn't give us energy, but about half of our body weight is water. Most water is in our cells. Without consuming water, we could only last for four or five days. The adult human body contains approximately 60 percent water. Water content can vary from a high 75 percent in a newborn infant to 45 percent in an obese person.

According to the Mayo Clinic, the average person should consume "eight 8-ounce glasses of fluid."[19] If you're thirsty and sometimes hungry, your body's telling you that you need more water. An excellent way to determine your fluid status is by the color of your urine. If your urine is light yellow, you're probably getting enough fluids. If it's dark or smells strong, you probably need more water. To make sure you are hydrated, drink fluids throughout the entire day. Consuming all sixty-four ounces in a small window will not keep you from being dehydrated.

Seventy-five percent of Americans are chronically dehydrated, and dehydration is a significant cause of headaches. When you become dehydrated, your brain tissue loses water, causing your brain to shrink and pull away from the skull. This triggers the pain receptors surrounding the brain, giving you a headache. Dehydration also causes your blood volume to drop, which in turn lowers the flow of blood and oxygen to the brain.

PEAK MAINTENANCE

Understanding your specific body mass index, weight level, and sleep patterns are all essential to peak performance. It is important to achieve your peak maintenance levels as well. Getting there is half the battle, but the other half is keeping it going on a regular basis.

BODY MASS INDEX (BMI)

Body mass index (BMI) is a measure of body fat based on height and weight that applies to adult men and women. The BMI is a measure to quantify the amount of tissue mass (muscle, fat, and bone) in an individual. This number categorizes a person as underweight, average weight, overweight, or obese.

The formula for body mass index (BMI) is the body mass or weight (kg) divided by the square of the body height (m). The unit of BMI is kg/m^2.

Calculate your BMI as follows:

Your Weight (lbs) / (Your Height (in.))^2 x 703

So, for example, if you are 5'8" (68") and weigh 180 pounds, you would calculate as follows:

(180 / (68 x 68)) x 703 = 27.37 BMI

BMI is a general index used to assess the physical body fat and/or mass index of an individual. The index is not necessarily good as a final tool for measuring health but is helpful for an average comparison of where you are and can be.

Commonly accepted BMI ranges are:

- under weight: 18.5 kg/m2
- normal weight: 18.5 to 25
- overweight: 25 to 30
- obese: over 30

Every pound of excess weight exerts about four pounds of extra pressure on the knees. So a person who is ten pounds overweight has forty pounds of extra pressure on his knees. If a person is one hundred pounds overweight, that is four hundred pounds of extra pressure on his knees. To live a 24K Life, these are areas that will help you position yourself to increase your health and therefore your performance. Once you are stable, well balanced, and healthy, you will perform at a higher level and improve your positive results.

SLEEP

Sleep directly affects the quality of your waking life. No other activity delivers so many benefits with almost no effort! Sleep isn't only a time when your body shuts off. While you rest, your brain stays busy, overseeing your maintenance that keeps your body running. Sleep impacts your . . .

- Productivity
- Emotional balance
- Creativity
- Physical vitality
- Weight

Without enough hours of sleep, you won't be able to work, learn, create, or communicate at a place that is even close to your true potential. According to the National Institutes of Health, the average adult sleeps less than seven hours per night.[20] The following is the amount of sleep we need:

- Newborn to two months old: 12–18 hours
- Three months to one year old: 14–15 hours
- One to three years old: 12–14 hours
- Three to five years old: 11–13 hours
- Five to twelve years old: 10–11 hours
- Twelve to seventeen years old: 8 1/2–10 hours
- Adults (eighteen and up): 7 1/2–9 hours

There is a difference between the amount of sleep you can get by on and the amount you need to function optimally. Sleep requirements vary for each of us, but if you're sleeping less than eight hours each night, chances are you are sleep-deprived.

You may be sleep deprived if you . . .

- need an alarm clock to wake up on time
- rely on the snooze button
- have a hard time getting out of bed in the morning
- feel sluggish in the afternoon
- get drowsy in meetings, lectures, or warm rooms

- get sleepy after heavy meals or when driving
- need to nap to get through the day
- fall asleep while watching TV or relaxing
- sleep in a lot on weekends
- fall asleep fast when going to bed

After reading this list, I know I have a sleep-deprivation problem because seven out of ten seem to be a norm for me. In order to improve and level up toward peak performance, I set on a path to incorporate several new bedtime habits:

1. Set a daily time for bed
2. Shut down all electronics at a certain time
3. Don't hang out on the bed during the day
4. Pray and meditate before bed

These habits have allowed me to increase the number of hours I sleep per night and minimize some of the bad habits and results such as feeling sluggish late afternoon. The change in habits wasn't easy but necessary. Changing things in my control that helps me create more personal power and operate at a peak level are not optional additions. They are mandatory.

"To think is easy. To act is hard. But the hardest thing in the world is to act in accordance with your thinking."

Goethe

The primary key to doing better is to know better. Once you know better, you can devise a plan to do better. Understanding your physical limitations and supporting your mental strength with your physical strength will take you so much closer to your peak performance. We all tend to focus on dealing with life as it hits us, but once we decide to hit first, things change. Part of leaving nothing to chance is preparing your body and mind to maintain a high level of activity without feeling tired, exhausted, or overrun.

CHAPTER 12
ALPHA LEADERSHIP

To be a great leader, you must have an alpha mindset. Simply put, you must be hungry for success because no one is going to hand it to you. The critical difference between being personally alpha and being an alpha leader is that there is far more ownership when you are considered a leader.

Leaders who put themselves out front, potentially risking their families and their futures, genuinely have to be 24K alpha masters. Most everyday people have trouble handling a regular alpha. Place leadership on top of that, and you will be viewed as a cocky son-of-a-bitch.

I am entirely invested in helping you dominate your world.

So many people operate safely in their secure mediocrity. I say let them revel in it. You need to be an alpha leader. We are looking to crush limiting beliefs, expand your understanding of your potential, and maximize your beliefs. The first move is to clearly know your mission, purpose, and path. Each of us is a leader in some way. The tough part is defining that purpose and building our lives of service from there.

What Is Your Life's Mission?

A mission statement is a proclamation of your real purpose and intent. I want to free people from the bondage of poor financial decision and planning. My mission is to help people desperate to be financially free find immediate solutions. Each and every one of us has a purpose, and many never flush theirs out. Clarify your intent with your mission statement. It's your mission. No one can tell you it's wrong. It just has to be pure and honest. Remember, you are fighting you for success, and it begins with knowing who you really are and what you really want.

My mission is:

____

____

____

____

Once you determine what you want, then you have to realize what you're honestly willing to do to get it.

What are you willing to do to accomplish your dreams?

____

____

____

____

Are you willing to give up sitting around for hours doing the following?

- Playing video games
- Watching TV
- Shopping

- Talking on your phone
- Hanging out
- Partying all night
- Casino

What does it take to be a successful leader?

- Being courageous
- Facing the fear
- Taking action
- Being a problem solver
- Being willing to help people
- Adding value
- Having a "never say die" spirit
- Having a clear vision
- Believing in your value

Without a clear purpose life is not quite as fulfilling. Deep inside we know we have a job to do or a service to deliver or a deed to accomplish. Once you identify yours, let your passion, grit, and vision take you to your greatest heights.

YOUR PASSION

People with passion have more confidence and create value for others by sharing their expertise. Confident people are usually great leaders and earn respect and trust from others. The reality is that passion is infectious. Being passionate makes those around you feel passionate as well, and everyone wins. When your team is excited and has bought into your passion, it creates synergistic excellence and a willingness to do more or go the extra mile. Your family, friends, customers, and loved ones will see and feel the value you bring.

Most people don't start with the idea or dream that they will be a leader. Real leaders just know a problem needs to be solved. Some of the most exceptional leaders have come to the forefront following a tragedy or loss. After some life-altering events, things become clearer and we can see a greater good in our lives. Tapping into that is extremely powerful.

I am driven to help people live a less stressed life. Living out my passion and my why results in families being closer, happier, healthier, and wealthier. If your life is balanced, meaning your mind, body, and money are all in order, would you and your family be in a more fulfilling place? Yes!

Power of purpose taps into the energy of determination and courage. You are clear about the mission at hand. You are focused like a laser. Your expectations rise, and the result is a massive increase in potential being tapped. A clear purpose or why enables you to focus your efforts on what matters most, pushing you to take risks regardless of obstacles.

> *"He who has a why can endure any how."*
> Frederick Nietzsche

Understanding your why is an essential step in figuring out how to achieve the dreams that excite you and to actually create a life you desire. There's no single path for uncovering your life's purpose; there are many ways you can gain insight into yourself.

Consider these questions:

1. What excites you?

I'm talking about a why that gets you out of bed and takes life from being about you to being about something greater than yourself. Life is best when it's connected with what you're passionate about or great at. It's motivating to know that when you focus your attention and skills, you grow your impact and influence on others in a positive way.

2. What is your natural zone?

Your zone is that sweet spot or point when your talent and skill meet your personal dream. When people are in their zone, they are more productive, and their work appears to happen with ease and joy. People who tend to make more money are happier because they have more options and choices!

What are the things you've always been good at?

- Are you creative and an out-of-the-box thinker?
- Do you love the details?
- Are you a great communicator?
- Are you a problem solver or change agent?
- Are you a natural caregiver or healer?

3. Where do you add the highest value?

Knowing your greatest strengths and where you can add the most value is vitally important. We often minimize our strengths, skills, and expertise to make others more comfortable. You must know your strengths and maximize them to add value to the world. Consider what problems you really enjoy solving and what problems you feel passionate about trying to solve. You'll then be more successful at focusing your energy on things you're good at than trying to bolster or eliminate your weaknesses.

Answering these few questions is a solid start to better understanding your leadership strengths and desires. In addition to these questions, you can dive into your personal mission. What part do you truly wish to play in the world?

Do You Have True Grit?

In addition to passion, you need grit. When times get tough, you must dig deep and manage the hurdles or circumstances. Fight your best all the way through to the top.

While passion may have initially ignited your dreams, tenacity or grit is what will keep you going. Author Angela Lee Duckworth, assistant professor of psychology at the University of Pennsylvania, considers true grit a highly relevant performance metric, just as critical as IQ. In her book Grit, she wrote:

"Grit is the tendency to sustain interest in and effort toward very long-term goals."

Angela Lee Duckworth

Everyone has some rich and lean years with turbulence at one time or another. Without the toughness to last, it is challenging to survive any prolonged periods of difficult times.[21] My mentor, John F. Savage, taught me to stand and stay the course. Recognize that change is inevitable and that a stern mindset and grit are critical to successfully navigating your plan to the top. Most times you can emerge from tough times stronger and even more capable.

As a leader, you have to be prepared to stand alone for a long, long time. Grit describes the undeniable nature of a person who is willing and able to go through any lengths and depths that would break the best of the best in some circumstances. Grit doesn't honor heritage, class, ability, skill, or sense. True grit is a heart thing that overcomes adversity in the grimiest of situations.

I am not exaggerating. If you are in a leadership position, you know what I'm talking about. If you are starting up, you will be faced with a question of personal grit, and you'll find out how much you have when you're faced with the dragon. I hope you dig deep.

You may have had past personal experiences that are an indication of what you are capable of handling, and that is a great place to start. In the past, if you have quit several projects without completing them, maybe leadership is not for you. If you have failed and decided not to try again, this may not be for you. If you had people talk you into the ground and left your position, this may not be for you.

Most people aren't born with thick skin; they grow it over time. Having thick skin is an essential thing in life. You need a thick skin not because it helps you not to care, but because it enables you to understand that most things only affect you because you allow them to hit you deep inside.

Just because you care doesn't mean you allow situations to have a negative impact on you or your perspective on life. Having thick skin is caring, but it also means you have the strength to keep pursuing what you believe to be right. Those with thick skin consider other people's opinions; however, in the end, their own opinion is what matters most.

Leaders with thick skin love their roles, but they aren't delusional. They know they make mistakes. If you're in a leadership position, failing the first time around is rough. Those with thick enough skin suck it up and keep going.

People with the thickest skin will fail over and over but will keep pushing forward. Somehow they will themselves to win. With time and consistency, the will to win becomes the habit of success. The beauty of never ceasing your pursuit is that eventually what looks hard to accomplish to the world is completed with ease by you. The ease with which you complete a task comes from years of setting your vision and future with conviction.

LEADERSHIP VISION

We have all heard that when the leader has no vision, the people perish. The reality is that your life will only be as good as the message you hold deep within your heart. Your vision of where you are and where you are going is 100 percent your responsibility. Your vision needs to be intertwined in your mission statement and your purpose. It may sound trivial, but if you don't believe in you, your life plan, or the direction of your path, you are screwed. The successful leader has to be ten steps ahead and ready to see around corners, under water, and through walls.

The traditional way to express vision is in and through your personal master plan. Most leaders don't write a plan because of the immense process and time involved. Setting your mind to it and tackling anything that gets you to your goal is doable, and you should never shy away from anything challenging. "If it were easy..." You know the rest.

"Success is not for the weak minded or half-hearted."
Derick Gant

Set up and layout your dreams. Detail them in a master plan. Cover every aspect of your vision, leaving no stone unturned. If you are creating something new, you can attack this in a few ways:

- Hire a coach to help you structure your plan
- Brain dump every idea of what you see coming together
- Get family and friends for input regarding your strengths
- Start with a smaller one-year plan and keep adding on

If you are feeling stuck and your growth is stagnant, you may have to do a complete reset. Start with a revised personal mission statement. Tear apart your purpose and search your heart before you begin to put all of the pieces back together again. Include in the plan spiritual, family, financial, physical, and mental achievements. The beauty is no one can tell you that your vision of your life is wrong. You just have to believe so strongly that no one can knock you off your journey.

WHAT IS EMOTIONAL INTELLIGENCE (EQ)?

The most useful tool for people looking to successfully work with others while being a leader is a solid measure of emotional equations or emotional intelligence. The ability to clearly communicate interpersonally is very crucial in our day-to-day lives. In many situations, your EQ is more important than your IQ.

Remember meeting that super smart person or having a genius in your classroom? Many of those people with a high IQ were brilliant but had extremely low EQ. They were known to be socially awkward. When we were kids we called EQ being street smart. Understanding how to deal with people on a sales or social level is vital for your success.

My advice to anyone looking to elevate and transform their lives is to develop the emotional intelligence skills required to understand and negotiate with others. When you have the capacity to understand people and what motivates them, you have achieved a solid level of emotional intelligence. If you don't have this ability, you need to focus and improve in these areas:

1. **Self-awareness.** The ability to recognize an emotion, especially your own, and understand its effects. This can also be seen as self-confidence, which is a sureness about your worth and abilities.

2. **Self-regulation.** The ability to control how long you allow an emotion to hang around. The goal is to shake off the shit and keep leveling up. You want to be adaptable, innovative, conscientious, and maintain self-control.

3. **Empathy.** The ability to perceive other people's feelings and to control how you respond to them. Empathy is important in anticipating what people are in need of and will help you better leverage your skills in working with them.

4. **Social skills.** The ability to clearly communicate on a wide spectrum. Today, people all over the world can connect at the speed of light. The boundaries of your message and intent can reach billions of people. It's vital when socially communicating to be clear, inspiring, open to diversity, and willing to lead or follow at times.

There is a need in society for followers as well as leaders. Every leader is following another leader at some level, I guarantee it. This being said, the mind and emotional connection leaders must have within themselves and with others is a very special. A leaders mindset is one that is built on extreme optimism and grit. The answer no is simply someone's misspelling of yes. A maybe is definitely a yes.

Your mindset has to be that there is no such thing as quit, no such feeling as too tired. Belief in your value and the delivery of your product or service has to be so deep that you cherish it above most else.

The leadership version of IQ and EQ isn't much different from individual EQ and IQ. If you have been a leader for a while, I am sure your IQ is sufficient to move you past the entry level. There is no doubt that IQ is vital individually as well as in leadership. You have to know yourself and the nature of people better than almost everyone. This means you understand how things work inside the mind and outside in the world. You should be keenly aware of how your style matches those you consistently deal with.

Your EQ accesses all of the psychology and communication courses you completed in school and the school of hard knocks. Think of leadership EQ as the totality of the technical information required to build, grow, and maintain your past and present relationships.

Understand how to grow your EQ even if it's not your strong suit. If you make and sell computers, but you are not a people person or consider yourself socially awkward, start beefing up on your emotional intelligence skills and hire a customer specialist because guess who is buying your products? People.

CHAPTER 13
FOCUSED EXPANSION

Having a personal life code and structuring yours for extraordinary success requires a delicate balance that keeps your energy centered and flowing productively. It takes dedication and discipline to understand and implement activities needed to live a fulfilling life. While my nature is to focus on financial matters, the mind, body, and spirit all factor equally into a balanced lifestyle. It is critical to understand that you have to work in each area with the same force and determination. I believe each of us has an area that we are naturally strong in and don't have to expend as much energy toward. This is a blessing because it leaves time and room to develop other areas that need more work and attention. Through developing these weaker points, we can become more successful at what we set our attention and focus toward.

Success can be defined in many ways. When you were growing up, perhaps food was scarce or utilities were often disconnected. Success for you may be defined as having a decent meal and lights on every night. Someone else may see success as accumulating lots of money or getting a PhD. As you look to build a 24K Life, you have to determine the size, strength, and intent of your purpose. If you want a mansion in Bel Air, you need a specific focus. If you are happy to have a small garden out back, then a smaller focus is in order and definitely appropriate.

The state of mind needed to transform your life is an undeniable commitment and desire to succeed. This may sound simple and easily attainable, but I assure you it takes extraordinary work. I desire to have six-pack abs, but I have to work my butt off to actually get two. For the bulk of our adult lives, most people are unwilling to give more than an average effort, which is why there are more mediocre people than there are exceptional ones. To be exceptional, focus must be a part of your life.

GET LASER FOCUSED

What you focus on expands. This sounds like a flippant statement, but it is the uncontested truth. Deciding what you want and where you want to be is critical because the result of not honing your attention in the right direction is inevitable failure. Ever get in the car and not know where you want to go? It's such a waste of time. To get to your destination, you have to know your destination.

When things are crappy, we like to close our eyes, not focus on anything at all, and say, "I'm good. It's cool. I'm just fine." People travel and buy shiny new things on credit all while they are suffering in silence. Not focusing causes people to be overweight, stressed out, frustrated, and fearful. The craziest thing is when people attribute some of their stress to looking at other folks on social media and how amazingly fun their lives are. What a load of crap. People are stressed out that other people are pretending to be happy, lying, or showing snapshots about how great their lives are. Put on your adult pants, look in the mirror, and take ownership of where you are. Commit to do whatever it takes to no longer be in that place. Know where you stand so you can start fresh on a different path.

Most of us realize we need to head in a new direction and are looking to develop a higher sense of self. The question is, are you willing to pay the price to get where you need to go? We live in a time of self-indulgence and immediate gratification. We finance purchases 180 days same as cash like the money is mystically going to appear in six months. We do this with our fitness, daily consumption choices, buying, and education. To improve our lives, we must work to curtail these tendencies and pull the instant-gratification plug. We must be willing to be disciplined and to be focused on reaping long-lasting dividends.

Do you know what you want to be? Who you want to be? What is your ultimate destination? Most people let mainstream media tell them what to think rather formulate their own thoughts based on their own discoveries or personal convictions. Would you rather be indoctrinated and conform with the masses, or stand apart and in your own truth? Many in society are reticent to step out on a limb and stand alone regarding their ideals and principles. They prefer to choose the path of least resistance. Determine your path and focus on the few things that will get you to your best self.

Success by RAS!

Proclaiming your success before you've actually achieved it is how you manifest it. The original Creator said, "Let there be . . ." and then there was ... until He was satisfied. Similarly, we, as creative beings, can create our own destinies. To put words into action with purpose and intent is the way we self-actualize. If you cannot convince yourself that something you want will happen, how can you expect anything to positively manifest? Many will read this and think, What's the big deal? Just change your bad habits and move on. Well, if creating focus and new habits is that easy for you, the rest of us are jealous. But we admire you as well.

There are scientific reasons why what you focus on expands. One known reason is because of our brain's reticular activating system (RAS), which serves as a filter between your conscious mind and your subconscious mind. Have you ever had a friend get a new car and bring it over to show you how awesome it is? You see the car, love the car, and you think you've never see a car that great. Shortly after that, as you go about your daily travels, you see your friend's car—same color, same style, same everything. Then all of a sudden you are seeing these cars are everywhere. Guess what? Those cars were always around, you just didn't see them. Your reticular activating system decided that particular car had meaning and now because it's important to you, your RAS brought it to your attention.

The RAS is in the core of your brain stem. It takes instructions from your conscious mind and passes them on to your subconscious mind. Because of this direct connection, commands can seep down into your subconscious mind, only to reappear at a later time. When you set your focus, you are marrying your subconscious mind with your conscious mind to make something happen. Send your reticular activating system a message that you are expecting an event to happen, with absolutely no room for uncertainty. Setting your focus prepares your subconscious mind and RAS to achieve your desired goal.

One way to set your focus and expand your success is by starting each day on purpose. Command your day or the day will command you.

Begin each day with a set morning ritual. A morning ritual is a powerful tool to automate your day's success. Each day have a plan for exercise, meditation, nutrition, and the things you need to accomplish that day. Thinking about doing all of the things as broad categories can feel overwhelming, but when you break things down into daily actions, you feel more powerful and in control.

The best way to break down broad categories is to have a specific goal for each one. Once you have a goal, you can determine what must happen today in order to keep you moving forward and stay on track for that particular goal. As an example, I have a goal to meditate for an hour a day as part of my morning routine. I break down my morning so I have an earlier rise time, but that doesn't solve my entire problem. The real issue is sitting in a meditative position for the full hour. I set a goal to add five additional minutes every two weeks until I reach the full hour comfortably.

End your day with the same focus that you started the day. Finish the day with a separate evening ritual that reviews, recalibrate, and refines your strategy. Daily rituals take away some of the chaos and distractions. People want to be productive but easily get lost in the daily minutia. Once you have your goals and plans, you can focus on implementing them and thus expanding your success.

CRUSHING IT

I have set many goals in my life, and it has always been the ones that were larger than life that I seem to accomplish. This is because I set myopic attention on the big goals. They consume my thoughts, actions, and intent. My certainty that I can and will accomplish the small goals called for far less attention and therefore actually might not be completed or accomplished.

The most meaningful goal in my life happened when I was just fifteen years old. My hardworking father pulled me aside and said, "Son, unless you get a full scholarship to college, you will have to work to pay for school because you are getting a degree, but we don't have the money to pay for it." I was only fifteen and definitely not mature enough to fully process what I had just heard with what little financial understanding I had. But I figured out enough that I knew he was saying that my life was in my hands and I'd better get to handling it.

I set a goal to get a full athletic scholarship to a Division I school by the time football and basketball seasons were over my senior year. Understand that at this point I was only a sophomore, and I had two and a half years of school remaining. Getting noticed by recruiters back then is not like it is now. There were no highlight reels or YouTube channels. There was no internet to reach out to schools or Twitter to boast touchdowns. Athletes had to stand out so much that he or she became the talk of the town. To accomplish my goal, I had to be myopically focused, or so I believed.

My life consisted of house chores, which were to be executed perfectly, college prep homework, reports, test, quizzes, going to school, practice, attending church two times a week, and going to choir rehearsal on Saturdays. That was the easy part. In my four years of high school, I never went to a school dance, an outside-school event, not even a prom. I never had a girlfriend or ever went out on a date. In all seriousness, when was I supposed to meet girls outside of church? My school was an all-boys academy, and my classmates met up with our sister school's girls at the sporting events I was participating in. I was so intent on becoming a scholarship football or basketball player that I made no room for anything else.

When you focus and work hard, Christmas can come early. By the end of the football season my junior year, I had received hundreds of letters, half of them offers for a full Division I football scholarship. By the end of basketball season my senior year, I had gained even more offers to play Division I basketball. Mission accomplished. Accomplishing this goal set me on a path to completely understanding what it takes to set and achieve real goals. Goals all have the same core necessities or they really aren't goals.

Setting Goals

Real goals have a measurable desired outcome, a start date, and an end date. They are also written down. Writing down your goals makes them stand out in your day. Write down your goals so they don't get lost in the shuffle and excitement of new problems, challenges, and decisions.

"Reduce your plan for writing. . . . The moment you complete this, you will have definitely given concrete form to the intangible desire."
Napoleon Hill

When you are preparing to set goals, pretend that you can do, be, or have anything. Let the hero that lies dormant inside you out. If you had everything in the world, what would you do? What would you set out to accomplish?

You are not committing yourself to everything you're thinking. You are considering everything possible. There will be time to separate out the crazy and absurd, but to start, just write down every idea you have. If you had three wishes, what would you ask for? If you expect little, you will receive little. So think big!

"The greater danger for most of us is not that our aim is too high and we miss it, but that it is too low and we hit it."
Michelangelo

Goal setting is just the first step in creating a life of continued success. Often goals are cast away within the first month of setting them. In order to prevent this from happening to you, here are some guidelines for creating goals that you will actually follow through on.

Goals should . . .

- be written down
- have a start date
- have an ending date
- possess a clear desire
- be positive
- be believable
- be measurable
- be reviewed three times daily

Most of all, your goals must be yours. You can't control anything outside of yourself. Many people set goals that are dependent on someone else's input or actions. The success of personal goals are solely dependent on what you and you alone can control.

In the 1960s, Edwin Lock put forward the goal-setting theory of motivation. This theory states that goal setting is inherently linked to task performance. Locke said setting specific and challenging goals, along with getting appropriate feedback, contribute to higher and better task performance. Goals indicate and give direction to a person about what needs to be done and how much effort is required to be delivered to be successful.

The essential features of goal-setting theory are as follows:

- Be willing to work toward attainment
- Clear, particular, and challenging goals are higher motivating factors than easy and vague goals
- Specific and clear goals lead to higher output and better performance
- Unambiguous and measurable goals with a deadline for completion avoid misunderstandings
- Goals should be realistic and challenging

Setting goals forces you to see yourself differently than you are right now. You see yourself driving an expensive car and living in a million-dollar home, but you still live in a small apartment. You see yourself graduating, but you're still in school. You see yourself making money, but you're still broke.

When you take a look at your life and decide that a significant change is required, you are challenging your inner reality of what is normal to your current existence. Remember, we are always fighting internally for what is status quo. This simply means when we decide to improve, we will be fighting our inner self every step of the way. Lasting improvement takes consistent effort and focus on making a transformational life change.

Be careful when setting goals because the mind adopts exactly what you consistently tell it. Have you heard of a team or person who has set a goal to get to the championship game? They achieve the goal and make it to the finals, but then they get clobbered. Why? The goal was to get to the championship, not win the championship. The mind will say, "Take a break now, you've met your objective. We are at the championship—mission accomplished." The whole idea is to set your goal through its completion.

"The same thinking that has led you to where you are is not going to lead you to where you want to go."
Albert Einstein

Remember that what you think about and focus on expands. The negative mind will grow and look for more negativity. This is why a negative mind will never attract a positive lifestyle. That's the job of the reticular activating system, to find and notice every and anything related to what you are perseverating about, good or bad.

Crushing your goals is not an easy undertaking, and I encourage you to determine how many goals you can successfully attack at one time. Remember that once you have clearly defined, articulated, and structured your goals, the RAS will jump into action. The reticular activating system will begin to continuously assist you in reaching your designated outcome. Owning your goals and considering yourself the master of your fate is the final step in getting what you set out to gain. Leaving your success in someone else's hands in a losing proposition.

CHAPTER 14
THE GREATEST STORY

What story? The one you have been telling yourself for years. You know, that lie you have come to love as the reason you're not hitting it over the fence. The one that ends with, "Well, I tried. If only . . ."

I had a great story, and I repeated it like it was folklore that had been handed down over the campfire for generations. The older I got, the more I added to it, confirming my foundation as having a perpetual "close but no cigar" kind of life. I will share it only to demonstrate how serious you have to be about facing yourself and changing your lie . . . I mean, story.

I grew up thinking we didn't have enough money. We lived

in a house where everyone had their own room (a big room), I had a hot meal three times a day, and I went to private schools, but I thought we were poor because my dad worked nonstop. He was a plumber for the local school district, but he would moonlight after work every day until ten or eleven o'clock at night, every night.

When I became old enough, I had to go with him on these jobs, and let me just say, being a plumber is shitty work. Literally. I was terrified of getting dirty when I was little, and by the time I was twelve this house-sewer thing was just mortifying.

We had everything we needed, so in reality we had enough money, but I didn't know that because no matter how hard my parents worked, there were times our water or electric would get turned off for nonpayment. Living in the dark for a day seems like a life tragedy when you're an impressionable kid. I didn't realize until I was older what had really been going on. Mismanagement of resources? Definitely. Poor? No way!

Anyway, my not-enough story held fast, and I was determined to get an athletic scholarship to break out of the cycle of not enough and because, as I mentioned, I knew that was my ticket to college. That or work really hard on a job and at school. The one offer I wanted was from Michigan State. I was the third receiver on their wish list. Of course, they signed their first and second pick, and I landed at Bowling Green State University, a great school.

Close, but not enough.

At BGSU, I would have been an all-world athlete had I not broke an ankle year one, tore a hamstring year two, and shredded my MCL/ACL (knee) year three.

Close, but not enough.

Because of these injuries, I quickly became a student first and an athlete second. I graduated with a communications and marketing degree within the four-year program, but no NFL contract.

Not even close to enough.

My story continued, and I became a very successful financial planner making and spending millions. For every dollar earned, I found a way to leverage it into even more expenses. You know, houses, cars, trips, private schools for kids. I kept producing in life, but missing my real mark.

Close, but not enough.

What changed? I decided I had to change my focus, and then I change my story! I realized we were never poor; my parents just had poor money management habits that had been handed down for many generations. As a professional money manager I help thousands of people just like my parents. I clearly see how erroneous choices land people in confining financial circumstances. In order to change my story, I had to admit that I hadn't actually given 100 percent in preparing for my sports and professional career. I was just making excuses as to why I had achieved a lot of my goals but never accomplished them to the absolute fullest.

It took immense focus and consistency, and most of all, belief in my ability to give all I have to make a new story. My new story is that I accomplish anything I put my mind and ability toward and I won't cease until it happens. I don't think about getting close enough anymore. It's an all in mindset, end of story. I had a burial service for that old story, and it has officially been laid to rest.

"With realization of one's own potential and self-confidence in one's ability, one can build a better world."

Dalai Lama

WHAT'S YOUR STORY?

I can't wait for you to get into your story. We all have a story, and it has been crafted and refined over a long time. Mary's story started when she was a little girl, when she successfully jumped off of the top of the garage over and over, landing on her feet, hands on her hips like Wonder Woman. Mary's parents were skeptical about her risk taking, but encouraged her with everything she tried to do, whether she was successful or not. She began to have successes and wins; hence, she expected this to continue in every aspect of her life, and it became the foundation of her life story.

Ralphie Mae, from the movie A Christmas Story, had a different start to his story. He wanted a Red Raider Rifle. He was bullied at school and led to believe he could never be competent enough to manage a toy gun safely. Santa put him down, and his teacher put him down; no one believed in Ralphie. Remarkably, Santa brought Ralphie the rifle for Christmas, and at his first opportunity, Ralphie nearly shot his eye. He was told a story, believed it, and it became who he was.

Your story is the summation of what you tell yourself when you're working, eating, playing, challenging, or just thinking about your life. Take a few minutes and begin to capsulize and evaluate your story. It sounds weird, but do it anyway. Decide if it's accurate or if it needs a massive overhaul.

How do you change your story when it's all you've known consciously or, more importantly, subconsciously all of your life?

It's not easy, but it is a necessary step in transforming into your 24K Life mindset. There are several vital steps in getting a solid 24K Life story. The first thing you have to do is write down your current story. You have to dissect what you believe about yourself.

> *"Think like a queen. A queen is not afraid to fail.*
> *Failure is another stepping-stone to greatness."*
> Oprah

Pull out a journal and begin to ask yourself what your strongest childhood memories are. You need to cover every significant stage up to your current life. Record how you think about yourself. How you react to success as well as failure. What do you think you add to a room full of people? Do you command attention, or are you cowering in the corner, trying to stay invisible? What words do you often use to describe yourself?

Remember to take a serious look at your vocabulary. I remind you that the average person has over sixty thousand thoughts in a day and speaks over ten thousand words. Imagine someone always putting words in your head all day that are harmful, fearful, or un-supportive. You would hopefully get rid of them immediately. But what if that someone is you? You need to fire your mindset, and the only way to know how is to pay extremely close attention to the words you use.

Recognize what you say to yourself when you make a mistake. How aggressive is the verbal lashing you unleash on yourself? Your inner voice should be your best friend encouraging you to remember the best about yourself and reminding you to tap into your inner greatness.

SELF-CONCEPT DEFINES YOUR STORY

You have to be aware of your self-concept. It rules your roost. Self-concept is a comprehensive view of yourself based on how you see yourself, value yourself, think about yourself, and feel about yourself. Self-concept is learned, which means it can be changed. Like any change, transforming the way you see yourself takes focused effort because most adults have already identified who they are and what they are all about.

The thing to remember is that your self-concept may not line up with reality. You may perceive yourself to be charming yet all the while you are just annoying people. Ask your friends to describe how they see you. Most people think less of themselves than others think of them.

Some examples of positive self-concepts include:

- A person sees himself as a wise person.

- A man perceives himself as an essential member of his community.

- A woman sees herself as an excellent spouse and friend.

- A person thinks of herself as a loving and caring person.

- A person views himself as a hardworking and knowledgeable.

Examples of those with negative self-concepts are:

- A person sees herself as stupid and slow.

- A man perceives himself as expendable and a burden on his community.

- A woman sees herself as a terrible spouse and friend.

- A person thinks of himself as a cold and unapproachable person.

- A person views herself as a lazy and incompetent employee.

We all have many of these stories running in the background of our heads. The strength of these stories promotes us at times and demotes us at others. Good or bad, you should become very familiar with your self-concept and decide if it's time for an overhaul.

"Yesterday is history, tomorrow is a mystery, today is a gift of God,
which is why we call it the present."
Bill Keane

We continually reflect on past events and try to assign meaning to them. We naturally think about our past and how it might be connected to something happening in our lives today. Our brains and story are so strong, we even alter or edit the facts over time to better fit what we think of ourselves. The reality is that it's not the story that's the problem. It's the message we take from the story. Therefore, be careful that you don't define yourself by the results of your story because you have the power to change it today.

Oprah once said, "When people tell you who they are, believe them." The reason this holds true is that whether their perceptions are real or not, people strive to be the person they believe themselves to be. We are a self-fulfilling prophecy machine. Our minds work overtime to make us into what we see, feel, hear, think, and believe.

Your Fight to Be You

The next major thing to be aware of when looking to adjust, recreate, and transform your story is your creative subconscious.

The creative subconscious is the part of the psyche that makes sure you are you at all times. It has three main jobs: to maintain your sanity, to create and drive energy, and to resolve conflict. The mind, more than anything, wants to know and trust itself. It would be strange if your truth seemed to change regularly.

The creative subconscious looks at your present self-image and makes sure your actions match it. This is why you cannot successfully break a bad habit until you change the way you think of yourself. For example, if you believe you cannot control your drinking, when you start to exhibit control, the creative subconscious will adjust your behavior to force you to act like your uncontrollable self and cause you to continue to drink. You can control yourself for a short period, but the creative subconscious will do everything in its power to correct your behavior so that your action matches your old version of reality.

To maintain your sanity, the creative subconscious will sabotage your success. You can stop this process by transforming your belief system. When your version of reality and the outside world do not match, you get frustrated. This, in turn, makes the creative subconscious want to fix the problem to eliminate frustration. Once you begin to transform your belief system, your creative subconscious will begin to work for you, not against you.

When you are not doing as well as you believe you should be, your creative subconscious will generate enough resources to solve the problem. This is why you should give a lot of thought about what you want to do. The creative subconscious will provide you with options once there is a conflict between what you want and what you actually have.

"The only thing that we will ever truly know is ourselves;
our personal being is our finest creation."
Kilroy J. Oldster

After slowly dissecting who I believed myself to be, listening to my words, and scrubbing my thoughts, I have created a new story. The CliffsNotes version is this: Derick is a fantastic person who understands that everyone and everything is where it is supposed to be. He is continually working to be his best self and deliver on his word. He is a winner, and he loves to see others winning with him.

Abundance and prosperity are flowing in his life, and he always gets what he needs when he needs it. Trying is not an option, and his concern is learning from the things that don't go his way. Derick is amazingly creative and exudes the insight and energy to see all projects through to the end with classic zeal.

I am continually monitoring my inner voice and my outer language. I test my self-concept against reality by periodically checking in with friends or asking myself the right questions. There is no voice more powerful than the one in our heads, and if it is allowed to run amok, unchecked, success will always be out of our reach. Reformat your brain, retrain your tongue, and master your mind. What is your new story going to be?

CHAPTER 15
WHO'S YOUR HERO?

If you haven't noticed, the most interesting things we learn or are attracted to show up in story form. We all love a good story. The cool part is we all have a story, and so the question becomes, who is the star of yours? Hopefully you are the superstar. Most people don't know the impact they are making because they don't see themselves as special or unique. If you think this way, that is exactly why you need to rewrite your story. Just image how much you could accomplish if you believed a little more in yourself? Stop comparing yourself to others and start comparing yourself to the you of yesterday. Just be better today, and that begins with you rewriting your story with you as the star.

"A hero is an ordinary individual who finds the strength to persevere and endure in spite of overwhelming obstacles."

Christopher Reeve

SETTING UP YOUR MOVIE

Every good story has a hero or heroine, and most stories follow a set pattern. I first heard of this pattern listening to Tony Robbins. Most stories are based on a three-act structure, which has been the pattern since Aristotle. The three acts include the beginning, the middle, and the end. Sounds simple, but each act has unique qualities that contribute to the overall story. Consider each one and incorporate them out as you rewrite your story.

ACT 1

The main character or hero is introduced, with the initial who, what, when, why, and where. The main character is living a normal, drab, subpar life. At some point early on, you find out the main character has a character flaw or a moral dilemma. Because of this flaw, he or she is presented with an initial obstacle that needs to be addressed.

Act 2

This is where the story speeds up and the real confrontation takes shape. In the second act the main character needs to achieve a goal as obstacles interfere. In the middle of Act 2, a significant barrier occurs that makes the hero's success damn near impossible. All of the stakes rise, and the hero must come face-to-face with their flaw. They are forced to make a decision to turn back and retreat into their past drudgery or to charge forward with the potential to fail miserably. At the end of Act 2, the story looks bleak. It appears the villain or obstacles may win.

Act 3

The final act is the conclusion of the story or the resolution. This is where the main character makes the decision to come out of the fog and conquer the demons or die trying to redeem themselves. This is the battle of the big climax, the triumphant victory. Finally, there is the happily ever after, or at least the glimpse of the hero moving forward.

A part of the 24K Life is about being the hero or heroine. There is very little value in being a side character in your own story. If you don't write your story, someone else will write it for you, and I promise you will not be the main character or hero. The beauty of this moment is that you get to decide what kind of hero you want to be.

PREPARE TO WRITE

You will likely have some issues seeing yourself in your own story unless you have a creative streak. Most people go with the flow and have a hard time getting away from their creative subconscious. Remember that pesky brain of yours keeps pulling you to who you are right now and have always been. It doesn't want you to change. It needs to know that who you are, who you were, and who you're going to be are always the same. To rewrite our story, we have to overcome that part of our brain, dominate it, and demand that it adapt to who we wish to become.

One of the ways to begin your creative storytelling process is to make sure you know all three of your acts. We can't be successful guessing how this story is going to end. You have to be able to see yourself clearly if you want to transform to live a 24K Life. The more you can see yourself living the dream, the more likely it is to happen.

As you prepare to write your story, get a view of what the whole arc of the story should look like. The process to begin is called creative visualization. After you have determined a goal and formed a plan, you then clear your mind and begin to walk through the entire process mentally. Visualize the first things you have to do to get your plan started. Feel the excitement, joy, or pain as realistically as you can. A good goal has daily action steps. See each day and imagine what it will be like to go through the days, months, or even years.

> *"All you need is the plan, the roadmap,*
> *and the courage to press on to your destination."*
> Earl Nightingale

Now that you have detailed the road, detail the victory. What are you wearing at your victory party? Imagine . . .

- Where are you?
- What are you doing?
- Who is with you celebrating?
- How will you celebrate?

- Will you make a speech?
- How does the victory feel?
- What are you thinking about that day?

The more details you create, the more realistic your vision will be and the more likely you will be standing at the top, hands raised in victory, with cameras flashing and capturing your greatness.

SEEING IS BELIEVING

As mentioned in chapter 3, visualization is nearly as powerful as performing the action. When you visualize yourself living in your dream home, your brain trains your body for that reality. This is not a mere suggestion. Olympic athletes hire sports psychologists to help them prepare, not to compete in the Olympics, but to win the gold medal. Players bust their butts to get to the Super Bowl while champions grind to win the Super Bowl. See the difference. Be a champion, and detail out your plans. When we imagine doing an activity, our brain actually sends signals to the rest of our body to complete the action.

A large part of seeing is creating your personal storyboard. Storyboarding is all about communicating your vision. Storyboards can help you construct your film, plan your shots and edits, and visually communicate what you want your world to resemble.

The process starts by finding images or illustrations that represent how you see yourself and how your story will progress. The next phase is to put the pictures in order of the direction you are looking to go to. You can actually draw these pictures or get real photos. I suggest you get real images. The more realistic you create your storyboard, the more you can see yourself as the hero, the more likely you will live out your stardom.

A popular version of storyboarding is creating a personal vision board. Visions boards usually start with a blank panel and then you gather images or pictures of the things you want in life. Vision boards force you to consider what you really want and focus on those things that matter to you. Creating a vision board helps you focus on what you really want. Deciding what to put on your vision board is vitally important. A vision board works as a constant visual reminder of what you are striving to achieve.

"Follow your bliss and the universe will open doors
where there were only walls."
Joseph Campbell

You have the power to transform your life. The changes you want won't happen by accident, so get to work devising the heroic victory you know you are capable of. Use the tools I have introduced to complete all three acts of your story in a clear and concise way. Think it, see it, feel it, and write it out daily until your images are your reality.

CHAPTER 16
YOU WERE NOT CREATED EQUAL

You are recreating or transforming yourself to live your best life. You have discovered that it takes an adjustment with focus, a new story, and a hero mindset to see yourself as a newly transformed leader moving toward your purpose and destiny. Most of this is a commonsense application that is easily accomplished with consistent practice. What's not so easy is to go against the grain on life concepts we have all been taught to live by.

In order to successfully transform your life, I have two concepts that I want to destroy to help your transformation process happen faster.

1. We are all created equal.
2. Being selfish is wrong.

"We hold these truths to be self-evident: that all men are created equal; that they are endowed by their Creator with certain unalienable rights; that among these are life, liberty, and the pursuit of happiness."
Thomas Jefferson

I am going to translate this in Derick speak: All of us came out of the same mold—white, black, Hispanic, Asian, or other—and because we are all human, we should all have the same rights. Past our human similarities and rights, we all have amazingly different skills, talents, and abilities. What comes along with being taught that we are all equal is the thought that it is wrong to want to be different or great, that no one is better than anyone else. We are encouraged to believe that we are all created equal. It's all a bunch of hogwash. The reality is some people have photographic memories, some are incredibly charming, while others have a genius mind for numbers. We are not all created equal. Your job is to discover your unique skills and gifts, then master them and exploit them. Utilize your talents, skills, and gifts for yourself and the greater good! It is your responsibility, dare I say obligation, to find your gift and be the best at it. The goal is to be so incredibly superior that the masses are seeking you out by any means possible.

"Always be yourself, express yourself, have faith in yourself, do not go out and look for a successful personality, and duplicate it."
Bruce Lee

The real point here is to recognize you are different from anyone else on the planet. Because you have different experiences, relationships, talents, and skills, you have to identify your uniqueness. The modern way to say this is to find your authentic voice and share your style and view with the world.

I wrote this book to encourage you to carve out a unique path to your greatness using age-old tools that have helped millions find personal success. I am in no way pushing you to use my specific methods other than to clearly show you there are principles or codes that you may be fighting that you need to embrace. *The 24K Life Code* is a guide to help you restructure your mind in order to master yourself and deliver your unique goods to the world for a substantial premium. Here is a great example of a principle that you must understand in order to be considered an expert at anything you choose.

10,000 Hours Rule

Becoming a master at anything takes thousands of hours, requiring intense and repetitive work. You will have to focus and practice your craft to find the secret to your success. The process of learning, however rewarding, is grueling enough to make you anxious, fearful, or even want to quit. At times the work you're putting in doesn't make sense. You may feel like you are chasing your tail, but in reality you are perfecting your game.

Malcolm Gladwell wrote a book called *Outliers* that states that anyone can master a skill with ten thousand hours of practice. The book has been challenged as inaccurate and studies say that only 30 percent of deliberate practice hours can be attributed to expertise.[22] The reality is that expertise doesn't happen overnight, and success is a principle law of cause and effect. The more you practice, the better you get. It doesn't matter what a scientist says, your unique skills, experience, knowledge, and desire to excel will dictate how fast you get to your desired destination.

We may have been created equally from the base mold, but it

is what we do day to day that separates us one from another. I may not have the ability to do gymnastics like Dominique Dawes, but I can manage and budget the shit out of her sponsorship proceeds. It's okay that we are all different.

This is the reason why you should never quit working on yourself or toward the things you want to accomplish. Success and mastery take a devoted, focused effort, and every time you stop and start, it's like you are beginning the first time. You feel as though you are constantly starting over because you have distorted your momentum and the law of forward motion. You can't break a fundamental law and think you can overcome it easily. You have to trust yourself and ignore the negative messages, people, or thoughts that speak to you in your darkest hours.

REBUILDING YOUR MACHINE

So how do you start readjusting the notion that we all are equal? The first step is to decide that you are once and for all ready to build your new mind. After your initial decision, commit to seeing it through no matter the price or the cost. Most people wish they had begun their transformational process years before they actually decided to start. Begin by taking radical ownership of your life. Once you do, the law of action will overtake you and drive you into your destiny.

The steps to beef up the machine are:

- Creating proper habits
- Setting great goals
- Setting proper expectations

CREATING PROPER HABITS

Habits are patterns we automatically repeat without any forethought or reminder. A habit is simply the way we live our lives, and there are good habits as well as bad habits. The habits we have are a direct reflection of who we are and what we are, as well as what others can expect from us on any given topic, position, or action. Rebuilding the machine means we must revisit our habits and determine which ones can stay and which ones must go. The truth is you can't get better unless your old habits are replaced with a new pattern. The length of time it takes to create a new pattern is murky. Most people have been told it takes three weeks or twenty-one days to create and implement a new habit or pattern. The twenty-one days to create a new habit is actually old school thinking and science. Today we know it takes a minimum of 66 to 285 days to create a new habit. The disparity in the length of time is based on the intensity of the new habit you are looking to create.

Our creative subconscious is operating in the mode of consistently bringing us back to our old selves. I think of any major change or creation of something new as a lifestyle change. Making this simple distinction in my head reminds me this is the new me, but this is the way things are going to be forever as I move forward. The trick here is to know yourself and what you need to do and say to yourself to get in a winning position. This is all about what you have accomplished in the past and what works for you as motivation and drive.

The most fantastic change I personally witnessed was in my father-in-law. For years and years he came home every day after work, walked into the house, pulled out a shot glass, and downed two shots. He did this before he said hello, how are you, or how was your day. One day after a doctor visit, he told the family the doctor had advised he stop drinking or plan for his burial. He never had another shot of alcohol. Crazy.

"Your beliefs become your thoughts, Your thoughts become your words, Your words become your actions, Your actions become your habits, Your habits become your values, Your values become your destiny."

Gandhi

Remember that habits are behaviors and actions that you repeat over and over with minimal thought. Habits are repeated so often they are done without thinking or focus. Get so consistent with your plans and actions that they become second nature. Once you have identified the habits you need to create, you have to set a goal to get them done.

SETTING GREAT GOALS

Transforming your life is a serious undertaking. You have to commit to yourself that you are going to be successful at mastering yourself no matter what it takes. You can begin by making a decision about what you will do daily, weekly, or monthly to accomplish your mission.

Goals have several common factors that must be a part of any plan. A goal without a beginning or an end is just a dream. Goals have to be believable. By far the most important factor is that you have to believe in your goals regardless of what other people think.

I've learned to tell very few other people anything about my goals. Believe it for yourself. When you put your goals out there, people judge the potential success based on their personal limitations. Their limitations are not your limitations, thank God.

Your 24K Life goals have to be measurable. Saying I want to lose some weight soon is not a goal. My classic reply to that statement is, "Okay, great. Skip lunch and dinner, and you will lose some weight." Goals are usually forgotten or dropped within the first three weeks of them being set. This is why only the strong survive. The weak talk a lot, think a lot, and act very little. Set your weight-loss goal at a specific amount, within a particular timeframe. Devise and implement a plan of attack on a daily basis. Set your plan to what you need to do today to be successful. Decide which exercise, what meals, what focus needs your attention today. You can handle one day at a time. You have a much better chance of success reducing your goals focal point toward just today.

BEING SELFISH IS RIGHT

The second life concept that I must destroy is that being selfish is always a bad thing. Almost everyone I know was taught to share, be nice, and not to be selfish. Not being selfish means you are fully considering others and being concerned with their wants and needs. The average person has over sixty thousand thoughts a day, and it is a known fact that the majority of our thoughts are about ourselves. By sheer nature we are thinking about ourselves and how circumstances affect our lives on a continual basis.

Being selfish is a skill that comes naturally to some and must be learned by others. When you are a giving person, it's tough to be selfish. Society tells us at an early age to do unto others as you would do unto yourself, and that's called the golden rule. Somewhere along the way things got twisted up in my mind and I thought the rule meant that I was to do for others, and if there was anything left, then you could then do for yourself. I have often wondered where I got this concept backward. I know there were messages I received as a child that shaped the way I thought about how I was supposed to take care of others, even at the expense of taking care of myself.

I always listened to my parents' uneasy conversations about money and the things the family needed. We never had any extra money, even though my dad worked twelve hours as a plumber every day but Sunday. Because these conversations seemed unceasing, I was always looking for ways to be invisible, and I definitely never asked for any money. In fact, what grew deep inside me was the sincere desire to please everyone just to make life better for everyone. That's a heavy load for a kid. I rarely asked for anything and jumped twice even when I was only asked to jump once. This behavior followed me most of my life. My therapist called it the good soldier syndrome.

I remember being sent to the corner store seven or eight blocks away for dinner supplies, only to return home and be instructed to return to the store because an item was left off of the grocery list. To be honest, that would have been an easy day. There were times I went to the store three or four times in one day.

The good soldier is ordered (not asked) to take a hill, conquer it, and return with the spoils of war. At times the good soldier succeeds and at times he fails. No matter the results, orders are orders: go and take the next hill. There is very little self in the good soldier so he or she just does what they are ordered to do. Learning to be selfish is just another necessary component of self-mastery.

"To be happy, we must not be too concerned with others."

Albert Camus

Being selfish is so underrated and has such a bad rap. We believe that if we put ourselves first we will do so at the demise of those around us. Fear of being selfish is a form of the scarcity mentality. But there is enough to go around. Don't believe that if you go after what you want that means someone else won't get what they want.

SELF-EXPECTATIONS

Finally, your self-care has to have a set level of expectations. You know what you believe, you have taken radical ownership, considered new habits, set new goals, and the only thing left is to understand what you expect to happen. Managing your expectations allows you to clearly determine what you need. When you know what you need, you can begin to formulate the means to consistently get those things and improve your life.

The secret with expectations is that they are set at your belief level. We don't really know what our potential is, so we expect results at what we believe our potential to be. This is why you have to understand your goals, habits, attitudes, and belief levels. It's also why you need to know what's possible. Have you ever read about a self-made millionaire or athlete who broke a record that hasn't been broken for years? As we looked at with Roger Bannister, when one person does something amazing, soon it becomes more prevalent. The belief that it can't be done is no longer a barrier. Set your expectations high and decide what you believe. Your actions will follow your beliefs, and the results will be in lockstep.

Your actions, beliefs, habits, goals, and transformation all require you to reorganize, dare I say reprioritize, your outlook on putting your unique self first. It is no mistake that we are all different on so many levels. We have the responsibility of taking our uniqueness and finding out how to apply it to bring forth our absolute best self to the world.

CHAPTER 17
BE 10 PERCENT MORE ASSERTIVE

"Ask, and it shall be given, seek and ye shall find, knock, and the door will be open unto you." If this is really true, why are so many people struggling and seemingly always coming up short? Why don't they just ask for more of what they want more often? I actually think there are two kinds of people: those who ask for the things they want and those who have thrown in the towel and resolved that they will never get what they want.

The people who ask for what they want fall into two categories as well. There are those who ask for what they want and get it and those who don't. The first is easy to understand, so let's talk about those who ask but don't get what they want. Usually these people come up short because they are not singularly focused, and because they are always asking for something different.

"If you don't know what you want, you will probably never get it."
Oliver Wendell Holmes Jr.

KNOW WHAT YOU WANT

Very little will happen if you don't ask for what you want, but when you are not focused on what you specifically wish, how can you ever really get it? People tend not to know what they truly want, so they seek out any and everything, trying to meet or fill a need.

Have you ever gone on and on about wanting to be debt-free or wanting more money? Sure you have, and shortly after that request, you fixate on getting a new car or taking a vacation.

To get what you want, you have to be like the people who ask for what they want and get it. These folks are clear on where they are, what they need, and what they want. Most importantly, they know there is a difference between wants and needs and understand how to differentiate between the two and ask for their needs first.

Their ask is never contradictory to their plans, and it usually lines up with their beliefs and feelings. Pulling these factors together creates a synergetic momentum that is undeniable. When you ask the right way with the right intentions, followed by massive action, things magically happen.

Once you have learned how to ask for what you need and want in a way that gets you results, the only thing left to do is to multiply your efforts exponentially.

DO TEN TIMES MORE

Have you ever noticed that people who have and get what they want are a little annoying? They seem like they have no issue sending their meal back or asking for a discount. These folks usually get what they ask for, and they have little issue with the negative attitude of those around them or of the recipient of the request.

I resolved to be more assertive over a year ago, and the results have been, well, amazing. It all started with acknowledging what I didn't want and completely focusing on what I did want. I would look for ways to be more assertive, asking for even little things I wanted versus feeling like I was being selfish or petty. Consistently asking for what you want is creating a new habit. Like any habit, the goal is to make asking a normal, ordinary action that automatically happens as part of daily life. The only way to do ten times more is to ask ten times as much. Pressing to do more and ask for more successfully worked in every aspect of my life.

I asked my team for more results and I asked my clients for testimonials. I didn't realize how little I was asking for until I got more. I learned that stores, satellite cable companies, and phone companies have set aside bargains and deals if you only ask for a better plan or more favorable terms.

Doing more in and of itself speaks volumes about your desire to level up. The key to asking for more is to be crystal clear about what more you are going to be asking for.

Ask More of Yourself

When you take inventory of your life and analyze your skill sets, you will find there are a lot of places that need your attention. To get ten times the results in the core areas of your life means that you must put in ten times more effort. To really see the results, you have to be very specific in the areas you increase your focus. Wherever your attention goes, those are the areas that will grow.

Consider the Pareto Principle, which we looked at earlier, when you are ready to maximize your rewards. The principle says that 80 percent of your results come from 20 percent of your efforts. If you deep dive into this, it means that you are wasting 80 percent of your time on nonsense.

The Pareto Principle has been vital in many areas of my life. I use it to determine which clients we work with, what clothes are in my closet, and how I grocery shop. Reducing the noise in my life and anything that is not adding to me becoming my best self has to be eliminated. The principle has never missed any mark that I applied it to. Using this in your own life will streamline the process of massive growth. What you focus on expands, so honing in on the significant areas of your life is key to reducing the clutter and getting to the core.

When you think you are at your maximum effort, you have a lot more to give. The best way to measure your personal output is to model someone who is doing what you wish to do and compare their efforts to yours. I will only model someone who has the results I'm looking for.

I watched Lee Iacocca when he was the big cheese at Chrysler Motor Company. He did some fantastic things and took some bold moves that turned the company from a flailing looser to a mega winner. I distinctly remember wondering how he could juggle so many things successfully. At some point, it was in the wind that he was getting a divorce after many years of marriage, and it was clear to me that bowling pin jugglers don't always catch that extra pin. He's a great man, and no one knows what happens behind closed doors, but I suspect that it's tough to be that busy and make everything work at a high level. I mention this not because I wouldn't model Mr. Iacocca. I say it because we all have to be aware of the cost of taking massive action. In order to live your best life, be certain to measure the risk and rewards. Living *The 24K Life Code* is assessing your truths, abilities, and skill sets at all times.

ASSUME CONSENT

I learned the beauty of assuming consent playing sports. Every sports team has a coach who has spent thousands of hours watching film, designing plays, and experimenting with tactics. Once the coach's master plan has been set, he teaches it to his assistant coaches and then to the players. The players are the ones who implement the coaches master plan during the game.

As a player, it is vital to know what the coach wants and to be in the right place at the right time. There were many times when the plays the coach designed didn't apply or I didn't remember his plan so I did the best I could. There were also countless times that I ran to the sidelines to be congratulated for a job well done after scoring a touchdown or a big basket, and was told, "Hey, great job, but that's not what you were supposed to do." Right after that comment, the next one was, "Are you ready to get back in there and do it again?" In life you will have a plan or a coach with a plan and as a player it's your job to implement it as best you can giving the best effort you have at all times.

Assuming consent or taking action and asking for permission later is an advantage the fearless have over you. While you are waiting for someone to read your email and give you a yes or no, someone else has completed the task and is getting new furniture for their corner office.

The key to assuming consent is to be so well informed and prepared that you will do a fantastic job. No room for failure with this strategy. When you are uncertain, make a decision and pull the trigger. People respect a display of strength. When you are unsure and move like you're walking on eggshells, people are equally unsure and begin to assume the worst.

"It is a mistake to look at someone who is self-assertive and say, 'It's easy for her, she has good self-esteem.' One of the ways you build self-esteem is by being self-assertive when it is not easy to do so. There are always times when self-assertiveness requires courage, no matter how high your self-esteem."

Nathaniel Branden

It's not your fault that you feel the need to ask for approval or consent to take action consistently. Society has protocols and agendas that are enforced throughout our lives. Look at our schools and military training; look at our religious ceremonies. All of these institutions condition us to act a certain way at a certain time as part of the modus operandi. These institutions don't want you asking why; they just want you to keep following along.

But you don't have to lead your life that way any longer. You can make a decision today to take a hard turn and start a new habit of making what you want out of your life. It's not easy to stand alone or to walk out on a ledge, and it's not easy to take charge and consistently make bold moves. But the more you do, the more comfortable you will get.

MAKE BOLD MOVES

The concept of assuming consent applies to the concept of exponentially increasing your activity and actions.

I clearly remember in my years as an eager investment consultant taking advantage of my fearless nature and willingness to do a little extra work. I was in a position once when a client asked me to restructure their portfolio because they were interested in making a killer real estate investment in a building downtown. After immediately completing their request, I did some snooping with the local planning commission. I was aware of several issues bubbling in the community that would likely not be well known for months to come. After my investigating turned out to be right on point, I engaged a commercial Realtor in a neighboring town to locate equal or better opportunities my client may be interested in. After a few weeks, I delivered a report to my client, who easily could have been offended that I explored his real estate interest. Turns out the exact opposite was the case. He was immensely grateful and ended up moving forward with the new deal to make a substantial investment. Our relationship was cemented for good!

"Never retreat. Never explain. Get it done and let them howl."

Benjamin Jowett

Assuming consent is a bold move that works very well for those who take radical ownership for their decisions and actions. I am well aware of the adage "assuming makes an ass out of you and me." Yes, it's possible that you may fail and end up with egg on your face. Even if this is the case, how will you make any massive moves if you stay in a safe corner waiting for someone else to tell you where to go? Be bold; be aggressive; be 24K!

CHAPTER 18
BE BIG-DEAL READY

Maximizng your business, activity, commitment, and focus will result in multiplying your gains. When the results you seek begin to manifest, you have to be ready. This may sound silly; however the life you're dreaming of and working toward will need a completely different person, a new you. Have you ever wondered how million dollar lottery winners end up broke?

The person who won millions of dollars is still the same person as they were before the windfall. They are unprepared for success and riches. Because the person is the same old hapless money manager but now they have more money, they view, think of, and handle money the same way they did before they had extra money. This leaves them poor and broke.

As an expert operating in strength and positivity, people will seek you out and depend on your expertise as well as your energy. If you are the best at what you do, the cost of doing business with you will not be a focal point, and you can demand your worth. We all can own our area of expertise and energy while helping others along the way. As you begin to perfect your skills and level up your abilities, it is vital to be ready for opportunities as they present themselves. Always be big-deal ready. You never know when opportunity will knock.

I took a job as an insurance salesman early in my career, and if you have ever been thrown into a 100 percent commission job, you know that they give you a desk, a phone, and a calling list, and that's about it. Ten guys are placed in a bullpen, and all you can do is sell your way out of it. The bullpen is one big area with ten to fifteen desks with telephones. Each office is separated by a divider, which means you have absolutely no privacy, and making calls might as well be on a community conference line.

To get out of the bullpen, you had to meet an annual sales quota. Between the massive turnover and lack of privacy, it was a tough place to get anything of substance done. So getting out was a big challenge. I am a very driven person, and failing is unacceptable. I came to work super early when it was quiet and stayed late to make private calls to potential clients. In our firm, we had one of the nation's leading insurance salesmen, and he was a wonder to watch in any meeting. He spent most of his time out of the office in high-power meetings or out of town on speaking engagements. When he was in the office, he would periodically grab a bullpen guy or junior agent and let them sit in on one of his meetings. This was a big deal and often lead to a commission split on a deal you had nothing to do with.

On several occasions, I was the recipient of this prize opportunity simply because I was ready and available. To be prepared, you simply had to be in the office, dressed professionally, and eager to learn. From my high school college prep days, I was groomed to wear a coat and tie every day, so that is what I did. I was always game time ready.

"The best preparation for tomorrow is doing your best today."
H. Jackson Brown Jr.

As I moved up in my expertise as an investment advisor, even today, I am always prepared to visit with a potential client or a drop in on a customer. The first impression made with a new client is incredibly important, so always be prepared to deliver your best at any given moment. I learned to consistently be at the top of my game.

EXPERTS ARE PREPARED

In order to succeed, you have to be ready at all times. Being hungover or late are sure signs that you don't intend to do anything significant. When you have a big fish or the possibility of a fish, you always take your pole, bait, and the best hook and line you have. Showing up off of your game is like saying, "I forgot the hook, but I have the bait, the pole, and the time," but you're still not going to catch anything to eat.

Being big-deal ready means you should be 24K all day. On your path toward becoming an expert, your array of weapons should always be sharp and prepared for battle. This starts every day with you organizing your thoughts, positioning your mind, and planning your day before the opening bell. Being big-deal ready means you look the part, walk the talk, and talk the walk. Know your strengths and avoid your weaknesses. Most people seem to be well versed in many areas and desire to be well balanced. The expert is a lethal surgeon in one or two areas and masters those well before moving on to any new ideas, ventures, or plans.

"I will prepare and some day my chance will come."
Abraham Lincoln

Every expert knows that the main competition is with the you of yesterday. That guy or gal from yesterday is a bum, someone to be defeated. The past is in the past. You have to be ready to perform and bring the magic today. Every day someone is looking to experience your gifts, and you should never rest on the fact that you were great yesterday. Keep your outlook positive and your habits on point. Without your habits that got you to the expert level, you will eventually be old news, just a has-been.

Every big deal starts as a little deal that was done flawlessly. The more small deals you successfully complete, the bigger deals the universe will trust you with. Prove to yourself and those around you that there is nothing you can't do within your wheelhouse. Be dependable for the things that make you unique and that make you great. No one intentionally pays for or ask for mediocre services or solutions. Everything great is the result of a process that someone with enough tenacity followed through on until it was amazing.

POSITIVE ATTITUDE

It's your attitude, not your altitude, that determines your path. Yes, you've heard this a million times, but are you applying it to your day-to-day life? To be big-deal ready you must have a positive attitude for no other reason than it's good for your health. If you understand that we are all energy and that energy promotes or demotes us, you have everything you need to know. *The 24K Life Code* is about improving yourself so you can have the best life that you can create. You are the creator of your world, and you get to choose to bring positive healing growth or destructive negative energy.

"Keep your face towards the sun and you cannot see the shadows."
Hellen Keller

A negative attitude has occasionally served me well in small doses. While playing competitive football or even basketball, I would see red anytime something unfair or vicious happened. At that point in the game, everything would get so tense and myopically focused that every ounce of energy went into my personal vengeance. The result of this maniacal focus was usually a surge of excellence that could light a city. This worked for me, but for some, it has the complete opposite effect. I have witnessed extremely talented individuals get mad and entirely fall apart. They focus so intently on revenge that they forget the rules, their teammates, and the fact that they are even playing a game.

Keeping a positive outlook is the smart move. Once you position your mind to see the good in as many things as possible, it's incredibly freeing. Look to make every situation a win-win by resolving that everyone will benefit. By becoming a higher thinker, you bring everyone into consideration, and people love to be considered. People think about themselves 95 percent of the time, so it's very comforting when they know others regard them as well.

"The person who sends out positive thoughts activates the world around him positively and draws back to himself positive results."

Norman Vincent Peale

My paternal grandmother gave me a copy of Norman Vincent

Peal's *Power of Positive Thinking* for my twentieth birthday. When you are twenty years old and in college, the last thing you want for your birthday is a book. However, The *Power of Positive Thinking* turned out to be one of the best gifts I have ever received in my entire life. The perspective and core values it illuminates is irreplaceable. When you look to be and stay big-deal ready, your mindset and approach to every situation become extremely important. I thought I was this amazingly happy-go-lucky thinker and had very few negative thoughts until I began to track my thoughts, words, and feelings. When you begin to track your thoughts, you will have to replace some of them with much better words.

SUPPORTIVE AFFIRMATIONS

Positive affirmations as I mentioned before are a great tool to use to remind yourself that you are on task or that you are capable of doing amazing things. As you look to be ready for any and every situation, you must tell yourself you are well equipped for anything coming your way. It is important to tie your affirmations to your goals. A 24K Life affirmation should be set in the present tense. The brain recognizes, "This is happening now, so let's make this happen." Your statements should also be positive. Saying things like, "I hope I'm ready because I usually forget something" is not a great affirmation in any way. Be sure to also add a strong "why" to your statements. "I always succeed when I work hard because it helps me and my family level up." My all-time favorite affirmation is, "Money constantly flows to me because every day in every way I'm getting better and better." Try it for yourself.

BUILT FORD TOUGH

I've noticed that in tough situations experts tend to pull positive affirmations and their inner story from deep within very quickly. I think this happens because experts have been in many difficult scenarios and survived. They may appear fearless, but the actuality of the situation is that from their history, knowledge, and experience they know that everything can be fixed, solved, or prevented.

"Opportunity does not waste time with those who are unprepared."
Idowu Koyenikan

Experts didn't come out of womb cool, calm, and confident. You build yourself through the fire of trial and error and never quitting. Being big-deal ready is part of the process of doing your homework and rolling up your sleeves. The reality is that when you get through to the next level, you have accumulated the tools, you have done the work, and you have leveled up.

It's imperative that you understand that it takes time to be ready to handle your big deal. I'm not concerned about you handling one deal; the concern is that you consistently show up and get many big deals. Don't rush the process because it is the journey that will prepare you to live your goals. *The 24K Life Code* is a lifestyle process, not a one-time activity to success. You have done the work, now it's time to go all in!

CHAPTER 19
PLAN TO GO ALL IN

After eleven years of living in our starter house, my then-wife decided it was time to level up and get a new home. After a lot of discussions and arm twisting, I agreed, and we began to put things in motion. The plan was to get that dream house. The first thing I did was analyze our financial situation to figure out how much home we could reasonably afford. That process included looking at our cash flow, spending habits, and cash on hand. I also had to figure out approximately how much equity we had in the current house that we could use toward the new home.

Once I got all of the numbers pulled together, I calculated the new maximum payment we would be willing to pay monthly and for how many years; however, just because I calculated the maximum didn't mean that was the number I planned on using. Now that I knew what we wanted to pay, I calculated how much that equated in terms of a total loan amount. That number plus the equity transfer minus a 20 percent deposit all added up to what neighborhood and house we could afford to buy.

Most people would run out and start looking for the new pad. That's obviously the next logical step, but it's not necessarily the best step. The right action was to test the plan. I sat down and explained what was required and what would change to get this new house. I wanted us to live as if we were making this new payment for three or four months, proving to ourselves we were serious and committed to the new plan. We agreed to consider the estimated increase in finances. The idea was to test and understand what we wanted would really feel like. We also needed to know what our commitment to a new home would be. With this information, we could factor in the cost of living and begin to save the increased amount for four months without touching it.

After saving the money for four months, I knew she was serious about getting the house, and we began to look for the new Gant manor. If I had been on my game fifteen years ago, I would have preplanned to level up and I would have known how much I wanted to spend on a house long before we had this discussion. If I had, I would have saved us a lot of work and uncomfortable conversations. The four months we saved money weren't easy, and I often had to remind everyone why we were doing things a new way. In the end, we managed to purchase an amazing house and handle it within the constraints we had planned.

"A man who does not plan long ahead will find trouble at his door."
Confucius

Having a plan can work very well for couples when they both agree on the path they are taking and planning on making. Planning removes some surprises and disappointments because you have thought most of it through. Plans also allow both of you to grow together, eliminating the imbalances that crush a lot of marriages.

LIVING "AS IF"

Living "as if" is a great tool that should be used as often as possible. Anytime you are considering making a significant change, it is beneficial to try it out. I believe it becomes critical when there is a considerable purchase involved. Living "as if" works in almost any scenario. When you are planning, consider what it will take to make a change and begin to see what those changes will feel like for an extended period.

This practice works wonders when you are setting a goal and you are not sure you can tolerate the action plan. Set up your criteria, and experiment with it until you get the right recipe. Once you know you can tolerate a change, you can finalize your goal, and it will be easier to stick to it.

I believe couples should have extensive conversations and specific plans together before marriage. Decide how you are going to handle the bills, the finances, the shopping, and the cleaning. One of you may be a slob or like to sleep with the television on. See how you can successfully manage together and then decide after a successful period to tie the knot forever.

If you are truly serious about making significant changes in your life, try it out. You might like it, and you may change your life forever.

"Few people have any next, they live from hand to mouth without a plan, and are always at the end of their line."
Ralph Waldo Emerson

MASTER PLAN

I believe everyone should have a master plan. A master plan is the full strategic layout of your story. Your heroic plan to live your life to the fullest in story form is now transposed into a plan from beginning to end. How many people wake up and have no idea what the day will bring or what to even expect of the day? This indeed leads to uncertainty of the week, the month, the year. Before you realize it, five years have passed, and you are in the same spot you've been in.

While reading this book, you should be considering and contemplating how the concepts can be compiled to create your own 24K Life Code. The beauty of *The 24K Life Code* is that it is uniquely yours.

Think of your master plan in terms of a far-reaching, comprehensive plan of action designed to guide your current actions for future gain. It presents a vision of the future with long-range goals and objectives for everything that will affect your success. Most people don't go to these extremes to secure their victory, which is why most people are not living the life they envision.

You need to make some hard decisions before you can create a master plan. Ask yourself:

- What is my purpose?
- What am I willing to do?
- Where do I need to improve?
- What do I truly want?
- What is my message to the world?
- Am I willing to go at it alone?
- What if they hate me?
- Am I in control of me?
- Am I committed to 110 percent?

These are just a few questions to get you started. Think about your answers and write down what your inner voice is saying to you right now. You have to know your purpose to set your master plan. To arrive at a destination, you have to put the address into the GPS, both the starting address and the ending point. If you don't, you will end up wherever you run out of gas.

Once you have done this, it's time to put together your master plan. The plan has several vital components.

Personal Time Line

The first rule of any goal is it must have a timeframe or it is just a dream. Your master plan is comprised of your major goals so the first move is to lay out a time line for how you see it unfolding. If possible, start at the point of accomplishing your master plan and work your way backward to today. This is called reverse engineering. Reverse engineering helps you clarify what it truly takes to accomplish your plan. Working your way back lets you define what needs to be done today to get what you want.

Part of my master plan is to create and deliver freeing financial content to millions of people across the globe. Part of this plan has me waking up every morning to an amazing view of an ocean sunrise. All of this will be done within the next three years.

Reverse engineering this has several major key components that must be addressed today. I started with the focus of delivering content to millions. In order to accomplish this, I needed to move beyond the one-on-one meetings and video conference calls. I formulated a message of financial freedom based on my years of expertise. I then started to create YouTube videos and online courses that can be accessed. Now I am writing daily to deliver an amazing book on how to level up and change your life. All of these daily activities increase my contact with people as I fine tune my message and people gravitate to it, share it, and reshare it. The strategy is to affect one thousand and that spreads into ten thousand, which exponentially continues to grow until I reach my goals or master plan.

KEY PLANNING STEPS

What are the things you need to accomplish your plan? Licenses, degrees, and certificates are all things that might be necessary depending on your desire. Identifying what key people or companies are required in your plans is also essential.

COUNTING THE COST

Every dream has a price tag. What will it cost to fund your life worth living? Most of the projects and small businesses that fail do so because they were severely underfunded. Making, investing, and saving enough money is always at top of the list of what you need to do to accomplish any goal. As you review your time line and the key steps you must take, consider the cost to each level.

NO PLAN B

Will Smith once said he has no plan B because it distracts him from plan A. Through the centuries there have been tales of fearless leaders traveling to a foreign land for battle, and once they reached the enemy's shores, they burned their boats. The idea was that they would conquer or die trying, and there was no going back. The ultimate implementation of only having one plan.

As a strategist, I have lived my life planning and re-planning. To think I only had one plan initially freaked me out. But the more I began listening and experimenting with the "burn your boats" theory, the more I liked it. I never set out to fail or get less than what I have planned for. You shouldn't either. Having no plan B is saying to yourself that you are going all in. There is no room for retreat.

One of the primary reasons this theory resonated with me was because I always knew I held back just a little bit from giving life my all. Even in sports, I would hold back during practice to make sure I had enough energy to successfully complete conditioning. Before I threw in all of my chips, I would think, What if I go all in and I lose? Losing will mean that everyone will know I'm not good enough. What a scary thought. Overcoming these thoughts is part of the process of adopting your new story, your new belief system, and your new action plan.

"Anything worth doing, is worth doing right."

Hunter S. Thompson

Planning to go all in is the best investment on yourself you can ever make. The reason for living "as if: and creating a master plan is to reduce the chance that your plan will fail. We may burn the boats, but it's only after we have created and committed to a time line, counted the cost of each move, and reviewed the key planning steps. When you plan to do something and you have done your homework, applied your experience, and assessed the possibilities, give it all the gas you have.

CHAPTER 20
GETTING IT AND KEEPING IT

The better you get at implementing *The 24K Life Code*, the more successes you will have. The whole goal and purpose of the code is to live your best life and level up. The success you seek will continuously come to you, and you will experience a fantastic life. As you level up and transform your life, it becomes easier to acquire the mindset, fitness, spirituality, financial, and material gains you are wanting. The danger is in getting complacent.

Everything you do or have has to keep expanding. In life we are either growing or reducing. We live a "use it or lose it" life. The lifestyle habits you are setting as well as the beliefs you are building must continue to grow and expand. Never forget that your new normal has been around for a significantly shorter period than your old normal. If you don't work to maintain your 24K Life Code, you could possibly slip back into your old normal. Think about how many years you spent in your old patterns and beliefs compared to the number you've spent in your newfound freedom.

A new client of mine had been working with me for just a few months. She had made significant progress in a short period and began to bask in her newfound successes. After a few more weeks of coaching, I continued to challenge her progress, and through several discussions, she made the comment, "I'm thrilled with who I am right now."

Based on the conversation, I translated this comment to mean that she didn't want to change and if she could just hover in her current space, that would be a perfect life in her opinion. I quickly asked her if how I translated her words was correct. She confirmed my understanding was accurate.

> *"When you stop growing you start dying."*
> William S. Burroughs

As a performance coach, I have to be considerate of what head space people are in and what their learning curve is. It is their curve, not mine, so we go at their pace. After digesting what she said, I simply asked why she came to work with me. She replied she had come to increase her gross income by 50 percent. I asked her if she was the same person she was three months ago. She replied, "Heavens no. I am so different is scares me at times."

I then proceeded to ask her if she could imagine being who she was today three months prior. Again she said no. The reality of who she had become and the habits she had established could barely be imagined, and therefore she couldn't perceive how much further she had to go. I began to help her understand that either she grows or reverts back to the business owner she had been.

Success comes when you put in the work, and it stays as you continue to work. You have to make change happen for yourself consistently. *The 24K Life Code* guides you on what to do and how to do it; you just have to keep it going for your greater good. It is important to implement and understand the law of momentum. This is an essential principle for continued success. You can use the tools discussed in this book to move your life to a higher high, and the same tools that get you there can keep you there.

THE ENERGY OF MOMENTUM

Momentum is a force that doesn't go away. In the world of physics, energy is continuously moving forward or transferred into a new direction. Never does it dissipate. Let things unfold and evolve in your life as momentum starts to accelerate. Ideas, connections, and opportunities come from places we didn't have anything to do with. Be open to the universe and the momentum you are creating.

Remember the last thing you decided you were going to do come hell or high water? It started with a whim or a thought, and the more you considered the idea, the more it grew. You started fixating on it, researching it, and making plans to secure it. You started the process and actively began to work on it regularly. The idea was more comfortable in your head, but you decided not to give in. The road seemed long, but as you kept moving forward, the object of your desire getting more and more apparent. You could see it, taste it, touch it, feel it in your possession.

Finally, you have what you want. You look at it in amazement, and it feels so good. You planned it, worked for it, and secured it. Looking back, you can detail the momentum that pulled you along the way and how the process didn't kill you but made you stronger.

You vividly remember the times you wanted to quit, but you were too far along to turn back or walk away. What may have seemed impossible was possible, and you were the one to make it happen. No one took on your burden and made you finish; it was all you.

As you marvel over time at your accomplishments, the momentum changes, and what you did either loses its luster or returns faster to its origins than expected. Before you can really get your head around it, the process is over and you have to start over again. You may wonder how you let yourself return to where you started. You definitely question if you can do it all over again. Tell yourself, "I did it once. I can do it again."

I'm not going to let you fall victim to the same pit I fell into time and again. The way to avoid moving backward or having to start over is to implement a recalibration and maintenance plan right alongside your master plan. Once you have the making of a grand plan laid out, you should know that things never pan out the way you have anticipated. They may turn out better or worse, but rarely do they turn out as planned.

"Our goals can only be reached through a vehicle of a plan, in which we must fervently believe, and upon which we must vigorously act. There is no other route to success."

Pablo Picasso

Stay Powered Up

When you are looking to keep growing, always remain open to new ideas, strategies, and tools that will support your plan. Be ready to reevaluate and eliminate those things that drag down your energy. As you level up, more people will naturally want to be around you, and while they are, they will plug into your power and feed or recharge their machine. You may not notice, but it is always the ones who regularly take who have no intention of giving. Pay attention, and you will see that you rarely feel better when you leave their presence. You may even feel worse or drained, like you just finished a workout. Surrounding yourself with positive energy and people who inspire or lift you up is like attracting like, and you will always be ready to engage in life.

Recalibrate Your Plan for Growth

You have your perfect picture and you are implementing *The*

24K Life Code on a daily basis. Plans are moving, and momentum is building. Recalibrating is taking the time to assess the results you have achieved to date and making adjustments as necessary. You are merely tweaking the plan and actions to land on the target you have in your mind. Recalibrating may even mean your activities are right-on but the aim is all wrong. Moving the target would never happen if you put your head down and pushed toward the goal. Keeping your head up, eyes focused, and mind clear is the best way to understand your destination in proximity to your current location.

It's easier to maintain and grow if you stay properly focused and motivated on your plan out of a strong sense of love or purpose. Staying hyped about something you love is really an amazing way to continue forward.

I don't believe in motivation per se as an appropriate long-term strategy for success. The perfect long-term strategy for success is creating that new habit. The habit will automatically keep you going because of your routine. Searching outside yourself for motivation is a great source of meaningful energy for shorter periods of time. But the person who is pushing you or pulling you will some-day have a mission of their own, and where will that leave you?

"Chains of habit are too light to be felt until
they are too heavy to be broken."
Warren Buffet

Basing your plan on your why or a life's purpose gives you a sustaining source of energy to move forward to complete and maintain your life's dreams. Self-masters get their own golden goose and the golden eggs. Have you ever witnessed someone who made something you thought was nearly impossible to do look easy? Of course you have. Have you ever asked them what the secret to their success was? They might reply that all you have to do is this simple action or series of steps and you too can accomplish the same. What they don't realize is that what comes naturally to them is nearly impossible for others even to conceive.

This is because they have picked something they are great at, love immensely, or encapsulates their life's purpose. Recalibrating actions will be a breeze under these circumstances. Just make sure you follow suit.

Getting it and keeping it is a powerful concept once you truly start to experience sustained success. This book is a serious look at the basic concepts you need to get and most importantly keep the life you think and dream of, your best life. I think I spent so much energy on getting it—fitness, finances, success in general—that I tuckered out at the keeping it part.

Be careful that you don't step back to admire all that you have done and then admire your results for too long. What you do and who you become is amazing and you deserve to enjoy the spoils. But the reality is that too much enjoyment and not enough work will have you reverting back and needing to start again. Avoid starting over by never ceasing. My fault was that I didn't keep working as I was admiring results. I fixed this problem by adding it to my core focus.

ADMIRING RESULTS WHILE WORKING

I honestly don't really admire results. I was forced to shut down once when I was hospitalized with blood clots. I had worn myself so thin without a break that my body and mind demanded a break. Basically I was forced to stop and admire all that I had accomplished. The time it took me to get re-energized and re-focused left me feeling like I had to start over because I had lost the momentum of maintenance and growth which frustrated me. Some people take vacations or have a hobby that removes them from the constant pursuit.

"If you're always racing to the next moment, what happens to the one you're in? Slow down and enjoy the moment you're in and live your life to the fullest." "Every single moment is your life, so enjoy the moment to enjoy your life fully." Enjoy the moment, this moment is your life.

Nanette Mathews

If you tend to never take a break, create a strategy to re-energize yourself as part of your maintenance plan.

CHAPTER 21
YOU CAN'T WIN ALONE

So what do you do with this information and how do you move your life forward? *The 24K Life Code* is the summation of the discoveries I have made and applied to my life over many years. I hope you will use this book as a reference guide to formulate your own personal code.

Transformation is a big commitment for anyone serious about change. Anytime something new enters into our lives, the unknown can be paralyzing, making the first step the hardest. What you have learned from reading *The 24K Life Code* is that it's not only the first step that is hard but so many steps after that. Our creative subconscious is continually working on getting us back to our core state, a familiar place that helps us retain our past identities. I would challenge you to start the process of journaling and identifying your strengths and weaknesses. Understand why you do what you do and where you came from. Take a look at your personal beliefs and determine your own deal breakers. Most importantly, be able to visualize your life in ten, twenty, or thirty years and begin to reverse engineer your daily steps to get there.

If you are still operating in the mindset that others are holding you back and someone is in the way of your growth, get your head in the game and start owning your shit. Wake up and stop playing small. Think big, be big, and big things will happen.

Four Personal Pillars

As much as I have promoted self-mastery and building your personal belief code, success is a team sport. No one is so prolific that they can tackle everything necessary to be great alone. We all need a team of people to fill in the gaps of what we are individually missing or might mostly overlook.

A vital component of being able to pick the right teammates and support system is first to master yourself and know what you need. It's crucial that you determine your own needs before you can assess any outside support or talent. You have to be clear on your own weaknesses and strengths. Picking the right people comes with knowing the areas you need assistance with in order for you to be successful.

Most of us need a variety of people who do specific things to help us become and achieve our absolute best self. Your team should be comprised of several key core members and specific next-level members, each specially selected to fill a need. Consider having these people on your journey to success.

A YES-MAN

Our self-esteem and ego can always use the support of a yes-man. We all need someone in our corner who has a similar belief in our vision and encourages us to reach for the stars. We need someone who delights in supporting and helping us imagine a bigger picture, a better life.

"We get up in the morning feeling tired. Sometimes we feel good,
sometimes bad, but we go through it with feeling.
That's the root to the truth, that's where everything starts."
Drew Bundini Brown

The greatest boxer of all time, Muhammad Ali, had Bundini Brown, his hype man, in his ear, reminding the Champ why he was the greatest. Being a hype man or yes-man was his only job, and he was prolific at it. The best sound to each of us is our own voice, and we can become our own Bundini Brown. Imagine, however, the belief and support of having someone in your ear reminding you of your past triumphs and future greatness. Get a great hype man.

A No-Man

Many great leaders fell from grace because their team only comprised of yes-men. It is crucial to have someone on your team who will remind you of the practical side of life, your plans, and your dreams. As success increases and our transformation elevates our view, perspectives can get cloudy. A no-man will keep you grounded and more centered, reminding you of who you are and how you achieved success. Having someone on the team who is not afraid to say no is a definite must.

A Questioner

Questioners are essential to help you think outside the box and help you expand. I have improved products and services significantly after reviewing packages with the team skeptic. At times it is the simple question that causes a deeper dive and more definite answers. As a creator maintaining an aggressive focus, questions can be the way to expand your thinking and test the integrity of your plans.

When you answer your skeptic's concerns, you inherently address issues your customers and clients will raise. Being able to overcome the problems in a controlled environment will prevent potentially massive public mistakes. This allows you to maintain your clarity and brand.

TRUTH TELLER

It seems evident that everyone should tell the truth, but let's be realistic: everyone has their own reality. We need someone who is going to do their best to clear away their own clutter and look at a problem or challenge objectively.

The truth teller is on the team, so they are in your corner; however, they just can't help but call circumstances as they see it. Their opinion may be in alignment with yours or against it, but they will tell you clearly what they think.

If you are lucky, you may find a person or two who can hold more than one of these positions. For each member of your team, the secret is to understand who they are and where they are on their personal journey. This will dictate where their heart is and therefore, the advice they offer.

Don't be surprised if you outgrow a team member who is not on a journey of self-discovery. Someone who sees and lives life based on how things used to be is not going to be very helpful to you.

Your Next-Level Team

Now that you have your core team, it's time to assemble your next-level team. Your next-level team is tasked with helping you not only get to the next level but to do it exponentially faster. These are the folks who add their self-mastery expertise to yours, and together you rise to do remarkable things.

Mentor

Every great talent has an advisor, trainer, or coach. We can all strive to learn on our own, but a mentor who understands where we were, where we are, and where we need to go makes success easier. Tapping into a resource that will quickly elevate your game, finances, and life is worth its weight in gold. Search for someone you resonate with and believe in. You must also know that person believes in you.

BRANDING SPECIALIST

What is your message to the world? What problem are you looking to solve and how is that best shared? We are very familiar with ourselves and our vision, but the way that is communicated may be different from what we think.

A branding specialist can see past the obvious and tap into commingling what you are trying to say with what others hear and see. They will help you determine who and what you are representing. Branding specialists are very good at keeping you and the brand on point. They will quickly remind you when you are on or off message.

PRIVATE ASSISTANT

The number one obstacle for most people is procrastination. If this happens to be a big problem for you, consider hiring a trusted assistant who will actively move your agenda forward. Imagine managing your dealings with a real right-hand person. The emails get out, the flowers get delivered, and papers get filed. Turn your thoughts into action by having a team member who can handle all the details that get you bogged down or that you ignore, and see the results multiply your success.

The Professional

Properly advancing your agenda will take legal and financial services as well as insurance coverage. You won't need these team members as often as others, but keep them on speed dial for your immediate access.

The professional team will help you get the funding you require to make big moves and protect yourself along the way. They can also serve as an essential resource to review deals to ascertain their validity.

Assembling your team may appear to be a chore. Once you begin to open up and review your existing network, many of these folks are right in your current circle. No matter the difficulty, always be on the lookout for additions to your team.

IF IT WERE EASY

I wish I could tell you that transforming yourself is going to be a breeze. The process of distilling down to the core of what is necessary to become who you want to be is a significant accomplishment, and it takes a tremendous amount of work. People talk about being self-aware and wanting more out of their lives but can't seem to crack the code.

Making *The 24K Life Code* a lifestyle choice is the best way to secure your personal success. When you make a decision, a lifestyle choice, you remove the pressure to get it done immediately. Lifestyle choices, by definition, are not quick-fix schemes. You are officially playing the long game and that is a recipe for success. Give yourself permission to gradually and consistently improve. Daily growth is the habit of champions, those operating at the highest level of their lives.

"Impossible is just a big word thrown around by small men who find it easier to live in the world they've been given than to explore the power they have to change it. Impossible is not a fact. It's an opinion. Impossible is not a declaration. It's a dare. Impossible is potential. Impossible is temporary. Impossible is nothing."

Muhammad Ali

By Any Means Necessary

So you are ready! Today is the day! You may have unanswered questions, but there is only one direction to go and it's forward. You have the fire, and you now see the vision over and over and over in your head. Get yourself healthy, because it takes energy to make a big difference in your life as well as the life of others. You've wanted to do better for a long time, so what's the difference now? You have finally decided you are going to do better by any means necessary.

People don't see the massive labor that goes into transformation, and you are not going to stop to care. Adopt a zero-tolerance policy toward your desire, steps, every action you take. No longer will you accept anything that goes against your personal code inside of your control. It's your season, your time, and nothing can be allowed to stand in your way. It's not what happens that determines your future; it's what you decide to do about it. Make the next year your year. Habits can change in sixty-six days, but lifestyles take a year. You are where you are by the decisions you make, and today is the day you are making new decisions.

If you change what's inside, you will see the results outside. Don't expect things to get easier, but do expect yourself to get stronger. Go to derickgant.com/myplaybook and start mapping out your next 365 days. Your goal is freedom. To get freedom you have to get your head game right, your money tight, and take ten times the action versus reacting. If all you did was take half of the principles in this book to heart and act on them, your life would change for the better. You can't get rich by demand, and health won't fall into your lap. Become more valuable intrinsically, and society will treat you like royalty. The call to your destiny is in your hands. Party later, play later, and pay the price to become the expert at yourself.

"When you hear me say "'by any means necessary,'" I mean exactly that. I believe in anything that is necessary to correct unjustconditions-political, economic, social, physical, anything that is necessary."

Malcolm X

Work harder on yourself than you do on your job, because your life depends on it. Your job will feed your stomach, but mastering yourself will feed your soul. You have the power to alter your life by altering your attitude. You know some will fail, but it is within your power to be the one out of a hundred who will succeed.

Turn your fear into your power. Do this by taking your master plan and taking one small daily step at a time. We discussed how unrealistic your fears can be. By any means necessary face every obstacle and be determined to overcome any roadblock. Your thoughts create your reality, so begin to focus on the immense success coming into your life. Those consistent small wins will convert into the freedom you seek.

Don't forget that we operate at our belief level, not our potential level. We act out of our deepest core subconscious beliefs. The law demands that we plant the proper seeds to produce the desired crops. Planting apple seeds will not produce oranges. You don't become what you want; you become what you believe. Think about where you are right now and that will clarify what your beliefs are. Accept that, analyze that, and make the aggressive change to your transform your life. Level up the words that are creating your reality, your destiny. You only live once, take the chance, invest in yourself, and don't be afraid to get outside the box.

How do you crack *The 24K Life Code*? One day at a time!

EPILOGUE
SPEAK INTO AND OVER YOUR LIFE

At times life seems to be uncertain. People are searching for a place to belong, a place to spread their wings and grow. Most importantly, people are looking for unconditional love and attention. Most people don't know where to start or what to do, and on the whole, life seems to be a mystery. No one has the single key to a great life, and no one knows the day or the hour they will take their last breath. What we do know is that a vast number of people have a deep desire to fulfill what can be called a life's purpose. A large percentage of the population feels a sense of drive and pull to birth their inner skills to help their fellow man also live a better life. The frustration happens when life gets in the way and clarity turns to confusion and fear.

Recently a very close friend of mine was describing how she feels daily. She is a professional educator and is extremely talented. She said she feels like she is always underwater. She is swimming toward the surface, and she is terrified she won't make it in enough time to save her life. The waves, currents, and tide are against her, and time is running out. She can see the surface light, but it seems so far away. She is all alone, and there's no one available to save her, and in some sense, someone has hold of her weighing her to the point that she cannot swim as fast as she knows she can. She feels like all she can do is frantically race to the top before it's too late.

I offered her a different perspective. Time is what we make it. No matter what age we are, right now is right where we are supposed to be. Our decisions and choices have landed us at this very spot. Many amazingly successful people found their stride much later in life, and she can use all of her years of swimming to conquer the water because she has become so strong. The path she wants is in her hands and her head. She needs to begin to create a new story and make new decisions and choices while understanding that time is not against her. She is not underwater but simply in a swimming pool, and all she needs to do is stand up. Stand up and realize that she is in the three-foot area, safe, sound, and able to maneuver in any direction she needs or wants.

Changing imagery helped calm her anxious breathing and soothed her panic and fear while allowing her to reframe her story quickly. With repetitive practice, she will see the pool and not the ocean. She will still be wet but not drowning and swimming against the tide. With practice, she will know that she may always be alone, but in that loneliness, she can stand and prosper.

It is your responsibility to speak positive energy into your life today. Today is the time you actually hear and dissect the words and thoughts, but it is you tomorrow that gains the benefits. You are consistently charged with the ability to be present, aware, confident, and strong so that you can speak into and over your life with the power to move mountains and overcome lions, tigers, and bears.

KARMA IS BEAUTY

Being present means that as you speak life into your present and future, you consider the good you do and who you are in charge of influencing. If you are a parent, it is your job to be the model that children look to hold as their future. *The 24K Life Code* is about allowing our greatness to pour out into the lives of those who are placed on our life's path. As you look to conceal your greatness, holding on to fear and uncertainty, you are denying thousands, possibly millions of the solutions to the problems you were born to solve. As you release your greatness, you give permission to others to release theirs, benefiting the entire world as karma swirls to enlighten and bring that greatness back to you in a completely different form.

For years I have provided free financial advice to thousands of people who couldn't or possibly wouldn't seek professional help. The majority of people I've served have benefited and even changed the direction of their path for the benefit of others. I cannot calculate the karmic return on all of the hours of expertise and professional time I've spent. The truth is I get underpaid on some clients and overpaid on others. Business comes from referrals from folks I have never helped or ever met. My success is built on the energy I was birthed to give the world regardless of compensation.

"Realize that everything connects to everything else."
Leonardo Da Vinci

If you can't understand the concept of you reap what you sow, you are a slow learner and most likely very selfish. The gifts we possess are just that: gifts. When you release fear and share what you have, it will come back to you multiplied. The more you give, the higher the multiple of return. Remember, the larger the problem you solve, the bigger the return you get. Big problems take big people, and the rewards can't help but be just as significant.

GIVE FREELY

This concept is shared and has been adopted by many of society's most successful citizens. Take notice of the largest icons in social media. They give away their secrets, their thoughts, and their strategies. You would think they are successful because they hold the genie in the bottle and you have to pay to get one of the three wishes. Not true. Just look and listen. They actually give it all way.

When you look at human nature, you will begin to see why giving your gifts and secret sauce away is a sure bet. When you give a valuable gift to the masses, they come to know who you are. The more they know of you, the more they want from you. The more they want from you, the more accepting they are of what else you have to offer and provide. As you continuously deliver, the hungrier they get and the more access they want.

Think about Tony Robbins. He freely offers hundreds of how-to videos on YouTube, yet people pay thousands of dollars to get closer to him at his private group events he holds across the world. Tickets range from $1,000 to $20,000. That sounds like a lot, doesn't it? It is well known that Tony personally mentors only seven clients a year and he charges them $1,000,000.00 each. Yes, that's correct. He charges them one million dollars each per year. People want to be close to the magic and are willing to pay the price to become great themselves.

Why would you hold back your gifts, talents, and skills? Prepare your mind, body, brand, and business to save the world. Share your gifts, and your gifts will bring you the life of your dreams and goals.

LOVE ABOVE ALL

I have told very few people this story out of the fear that people would think I was crazy. I was at a time in my life when everything was moving super fast because I was pressing against the universe. The harder I pushed, the busier I got, and the more things began to happen. One day I was teaching a spin class, like I had done a thousand times before.

This particular 6:00 a.m. class my shoulder was hurting, and like a typical guy, I shrugged it off. Halfway through spin class, I was out of breath. As I have mentioned, I am incredibly competitive, so I refused to let the class think they were outperforming me and pushed even harder. The class ended, and I limped to the shower, out of breath, and though I was unable to lift my arm above my head, I went to work.

My breath never fully recovered, and I began to pant. Each breath felt like someone was sticking a small sharp knife into my side. I worked all morning and met a client and friend for a business lunch. I figured I had heartburn so I ordered a Coke with the hopes that a really good burp would end all this nonsense. It didn't.

To make a long story short, I ended up having a blood clot in my lungs and being hospitalized for seven days. During my visit, which felt more like a jail sentence, I replayed my life history and had a conversation with God (the cray-cray part). I swear I wasn't praying, and this was a legit conversation. God asked me about my time on earth and about my life. I anxiously shared all of my triumphs as a good son, father, husband, church member, good Samaritan, financial advisor, and an all-around great guy. He replied and said, "What else did you do?"

I was shocked that God was hard of hearing, but hey, He may have been distracted with eight billion people and who knows how many universes to manage. I happily repeated every word, and He said, "Hey, I heard you the first time. What else did you do?"

It scared the shit out of me.. I didn't have anything to say so I prayed that He would show me what I was missing and was sent here to do. Here is what I said: "Lord, I will do anything you say, but please don't make me learn anything new. Lord, can you use something I can already do?"

I didn't get an immediate answer, so I did what I knew to do: start focusing and planning to make a meaningful life adjustment. Here's what happened:

1. I created a personal mission statement.
2. I kept working, but I did a massive brain dump of possibilities.
3. I got my answer in less than three months.
4. I worked my existing career and started the new venture right away.

My mission statement was and is to manifest a positive financial change in people's lives who need and desire help. Up to this date, I had given free advice to the needy, but my focus was to make wealthy people richer. I would continue to do that, but now I would truly help people who needed help, not people who just wanted to get richer.

I spearheaded a financial system that has helped thousands fix their financial woes and saved hundreds, if not thousands of financial arguments between spouses. Even though my team and I make money helping people financially, we also gave away hundreds of thousands of dollars in services over the years. It is our ministry and my ticket into heaven.

I share this transformational story to show you that even when you think you are on the right path, you have to be open to the momentum of where life is taking you. Even during this enlightenment, I still searched for the final answer to my personal why.

I have been journaling since my college years, and like anything you do repeatedly, I got better at it. Through struggles and triumphs, I searched for my why, and after a long process, I came up with the obvious.

As an ex-athlete, I always assumed my drive was because I am mad-crazy competitive with most things. I compete against kids, adults, animals, ideas, history, analytics. You name it, I have challenged it. But the competition wasn't my answer. As a financial advisor, I manage money, talk about money every day, and believe money is energy and that energy can move mountains. I rationalize that money as energy can buy me choices and options and that having these fantastic choices and options will provide me financial freedom. Believe me when I say that for years, I preached financial freedom as the means to the end, and the end for me was freedom. Freedom means that I can come and go when I like, how I like, as often as I like, no matter the time or cost.

I honestly thought my why was freedom. But the truth is, my why is love. I desire to give love and receive love unconditionally.

"Unconditional love is the greatest gift of all."
Sylvia Massara

One day my mother called me out of the blue. I was going through a very tough time in life, and she said to me, "Derick, there is nothing you can do in this life that will deter my love for you." After I wiped the tears from my eyes, I could better understand unconditional love. I'm not saying she loved me unconditionally; I'm saying her love was as close as I believe we can get. No matter what

I have on my vision board, in master plan, or in my heart, it all lands in a desire to love unconditionally.

Imagine a world where everyone was living their gifts to the fullest and sharing them. There would be no need for money, no lack or shortage of anything, and everyone would add and take the value as needed no questions asked.

I have put in the work analyzing my strengths, weaknesses, my goals, dreams, and most importantly, my why. I am sharing my gifts, and *The 24K Life Code* so that you may find your gifts and the courage to share them with the world. We are waiting.

"Be Your Best, Bring Your Best, Leave Nothing to Chance."

Derick Gant

ENDNOTES

1 Author Unknown, 12 Immutable laws, https://lawsoftheuniverse.
weebly.com/law-of-action.html accessed March 2019

2 American Stress Institute, America's #1 Health Problem, 1983
https://www.stress.org/americas-1-health-problem

3 Don Joseph Goewey, The End of Stress, Four Steps to Rewire Your
Brain.
08/25/2015 https://www.huffpost.com/entry/85-of-what-we-worry-
about_b_8028368

4 Merriam-Webster https://www.merriam-webster.com/dictionary/
discipline

5 Phillippa Lally, How Habits are Formed. *The European Journal of
Social Psychology*, July 2009

6 Dale Carnegie, *How to Win Friends and Influence People* published in
1936

7 National Science Foundation published an article summarizing research on human thoughts per day. 2005 https://www.nsf.gov/news/
news_summ.jsp?cntn_id=105693

8 Lev Vygotsky (1896–1934) zone of proximal development 1931,
various studies.

9 Socratic Method, Merriam Webster https://www.merriam-webster.
com/dictionary/Socratic%20method

10 Vilfredo Pareto, who noted the 80/20 connection while at the University of Lausanne in 1896, as published in his first work, Cours d'économie politique.

11 National Heart, Lung, and Blood Institute (NHLBI) Study links irregular sleep patterns to metabolic disorders, June 5, 2019 https://www.nhlbi.nih.gov/news/2019/study-links-irregular-sleep-patterns-metabolic-disorders

12 Anthony Robbins *Unlimited Power: The New Science of Personal Achievement*, Free Press Simon and Schuster 1986

13 Gary Keller, *The One Thing: The Surprisingly Simple Truth Behind Extraordinary Results Texas*, Bard Press 2013

14 Kif Leswing How Big companies like Google and Facebook set salaries. Published Sat, Jun 15 20199:30 AM EDT
Pay Scale https://www.payscale.com/research/US/Employer=-Google%2C_Inc./Salary

15 Ben Endley Addicted to electronics: Published: 11:26 EST, 6 March 2014 | Updated: 12:36 EST, 6 March 2014 https://www.dailymail.co.uk/news/article-2574823/American-adults-spend-half-day-electronic-media-including-five-hours-TV-hour-smart-phone.html

16 World Internet Statistics April 2019, https://www.internetworldstats.com/stats.htm

17 David Goggins, *Cant Hurt Me: Master Your Mind and Defy the Odds*, Lioncrest Publishing 2018

18 S. Sobolewski, A. C. K. Lawrence, and P. Bagshaw, Human nails and body iron Journal of Clinical Pathology, 1978, 31, 1068-1072

19 Mayo Clinic Health Systems, Water Essential to your body, June 18, 2019 https://www.mayoclinichealthsystem.org/hometown-health/speaking-of-health/water-essential-to-your-body

20 National Heart, Lung, and Blood Institute (NHLBI) Study links irregular sleep patterns to metabolic disorders, June 5, 2019 https://www.nhlbi.nih.gov/news/2019/study-links-irregular-sleep-patterns-metabolic-disorders

21 Angela Lee Duckworth, *Grit The Power of Passion and Perseverance*, Simon and Schuster, Inc. May 3, 2016

22 Hambrick, Oswald, Altmann, Meinz, Gobet, & Campitelli, Acquiring Expertise: Ability, Practice, and Other Influences Volume 45, 2014

ABOUT THE AUTHOR

DERICK GANT is an author, a 2-time TEDx speaker, financial expert, and high performance coach with almost 30 years of entrepreneurial experience. As an expert coach and fitness guru, Derick takes complicated concepts and delivers them in understandable terms. His well-known mantra *"Master you mind and you will always be free"* has enabled him to achieve mental, physical ,and financial abundance in his own life. You may have caught Derick on CBS, NBC, ABC, Fox News, or TEDx sharing his tips with millions of people on not only how to make money, but how to grow and keep it. Through his programs, books, and videos, Derick empowers others to break through barriers in order to have a bigger vision for themselves and live out their dreams.

Derick currently runs 24K Life, a community that provides high achievers with solutions and strategies to help them raise their standards to deliver their best by removing limiting beliefs and habits that hold them back, create a lifestyle that includes mastery in all areas, and empower them to become the best version of themselves.

CONNECT WITH DERICK

 @DERICKGANT

 @DERICKLGANT

 DERICK GANT

 DERICKGANT.COM

START YOUR 24K LIFE TODAY

Start mapping out your next 365 days. Your goal is freedom. To get freedom you have to get your head game right, your money tight, and take ten times your current action.

GO TO DERICKGANT.COM/MYPLAYBOOK

TRANSFORM YOUR

- MINDSET
- BODY
- MONEY
- RELATIONSHIPS

GET YOUR ACCESS TO

- 24K LIFE DAILY PLANNER
- PRIVATE COACHING LAUNCH CODE
- ACCESS TO THE DIGITAL LIBRARY
- 24K LIFE CODE COMMUNITY

JOIN THE 24K NATION PRIVATE COMMUNITY

Where high-achievers live, learn, and earn. 24K Nation is a community of individuals, entrepreneurs, and professionals gathered to live, learn, and earn their best life possible. We strive to live the 24K Life, being simply the best, every day as a way of life.

WWW.JOINDERICK.COM

www.ingramcontent.com/pod-product-compliance
Lightning Source LLC
Chambersburg PA
CBHW051755050726
47598CB00006B/2292